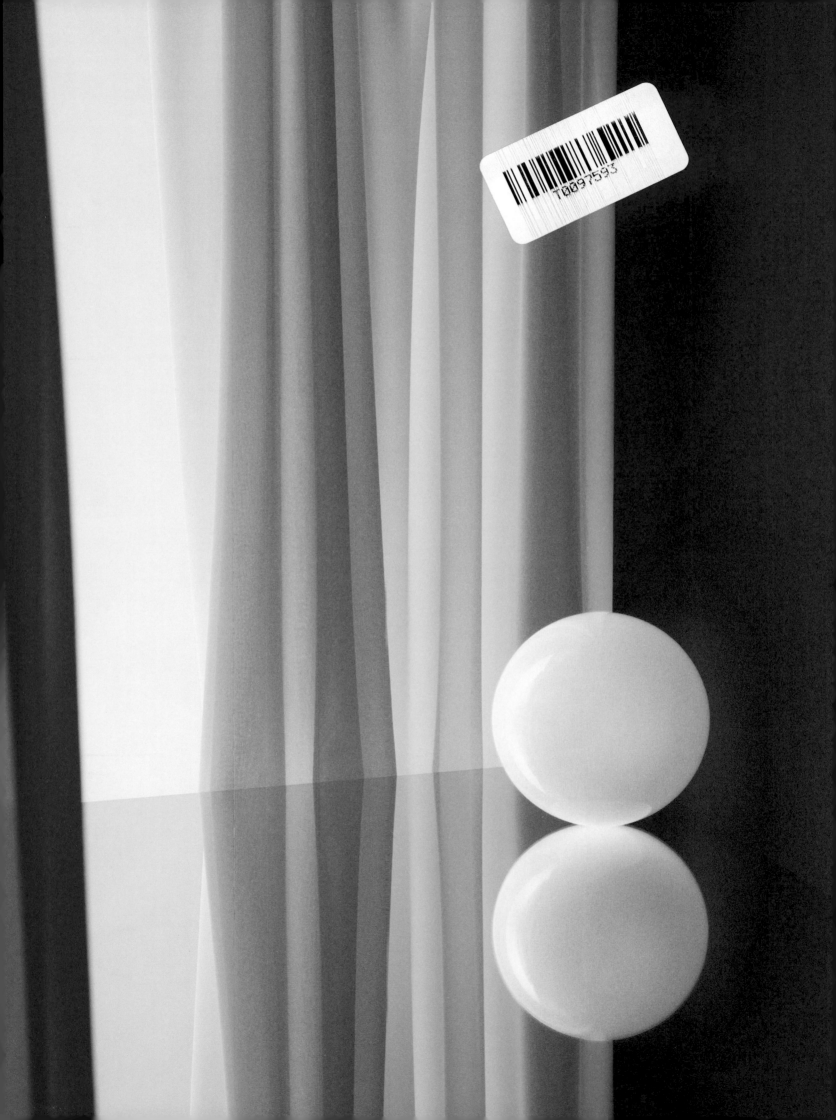

T0097593

PARACHUTE

LOS ANGELES | NEW YORK | SAN FRANCISCO | PORTLAND

PARACHUTEHOME.COM

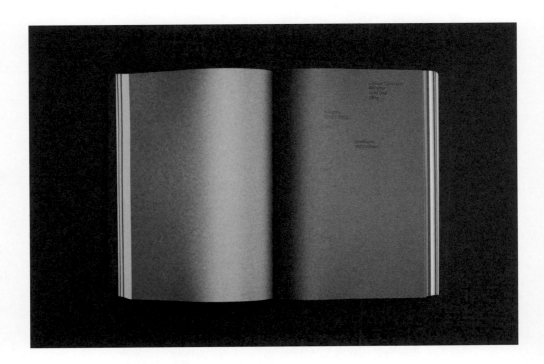

Curious Alchemy
An innovation in paper science

arjowigginscreativepapers.com

Weights:
0g / 300g

Envelopes:
160x160mm

our rugs lie lightly on this earth

armadillo-co.com

To be bold is to be true to your nature

marimekko

Art of print making since 1951

Flagship stores: Helsinki – New York – Tokyo – Sydney – Stockholm – marimekko.com

Tina Frey Designs
tf.design

Modern Designs in Resin

tf

danish design by · made by

marset

Dipping Light by Jordi Canudas
Taking care of light

KINFOLK

FOUNDER & CREATIVE DIRECTOR
Nathan Williams

EDITOR-IN-CHIEF
John Clifford Burns

EDITOR
Harriet Fitch Little

ART DIRECTOR
Christian Møller Andersen

DESIGN DIRECTOR
Alex Hunting

BRAND DIRECTOR
Amy Woodroffe

COPY EDITOR
Rachel Holzman

COMMUNICATIONS DIRECTOR
Jessica Gray

PRODUCER
Cecilie Jegsen

PROJECT MANAGER
Garett Nelson

CASTING DIRECTOR
Sarah Bunter

**SALES & DISTRIBUTION
DIRECTOR**
Frédéric Mähl

**BUSINESS OPERATIONS
MANAGER**
Kasper Schademan

STUDIO MANAGER
Aryana Tajdivand-Echevarria

EDITORIAL ASSISTANTS
Sylva Bocşa
Ulrika Lukševica

CONTRIBUTING EDITORS
Michael Anastassiades
Jonas Bjerre-Poulsen
Andrea Codrington Lippke
Ilse Crawford
Margot Henderson
Leonard Koren
Hans Ulrich Obrist
Amy Sall
Matt Willey

WORDS
Rima Sabina Aouf
Alex Anderson
Elise Bell
Jonas Bjerre-Poulsen
Ellie Violet Bramley
John Clifford Burns
Katie Calautti
Stephanie d'Arc Taylor
Djassi DaCosta Johnson
Cody Delistraty
Daphnée Denis
Harriet Fitch Little
Tahirah Hairston
Nikolaj Hansson
Oliver Hugemark
Hugo Macdonald
Sala Elise Patterson
Debika Ray
Asher Ross
Neda Semnani
Charles Shafaieh
Ben Shattuck
Pip Usher
Laura Waddell

CROSSWORD
Molly Young

STYLING, HAIR & MAKEUP
Ashley Abtahie
Matilda Beckman
Ashleigh Ciucci
Taan Doan
Keiko Hamaguchi
Debbie Hsieh
Lisa Jahovic
Cyril Laine
Katie Mellinger
Clay Nielson
Claire Plekhoff
Camille-Joséphine Teisseire

PHOTOGRAPHY
Gustav Almestål
Laurynas Aravicius
Matthew Attard Navarro
Claire Benoist
Manuel Bougot
Luc Braquet
Claire Cottrell
Christopher Ferguson
Jean-Marie Franceschi
Mary Gaudin
Gabriela Hasbun
Robert W. Kelley
Lorenz Kienzle
Heinz Kluetmeier
Romain Laprade
Mon Levchenkova
Katie McCurdy
Christian Møller Andersen
Benoit Paillé
Kenzo Tange
Aaron Tilley
Zoltan Tombor
Frederik Vercruysse
Verner Panton Design
Alexander Wolfe

PUBLICATION DESIGN
Alex Hunting Studio

ISSUE 31

info@kinfolk.com
www.kinfolk.com

Published by Ouur Media
Amagertorv 14, Level 1
1160 Copenhagen, Denmark

The views expressed in Kinfolk magazine are those of the respective contributors and are not necessarily shared by the company or its staff.

SUBSCRIBE
Kinfolk is published four times a year. To subscribe, visit kinfolk.com/subscribe or email us at info@kinfolk.com

CONTACT US
If you have questions or comments, please write to us at info@kinfolk.com. For advertising inquiries, get in touch at advertising@kinfolk.com

23.05.19 – 07.06.19

Join us during 3 Days of Design at The Kinfolk Gallery in Copenhagen for the launch of a
new furniture collection by Norm Architects, Keiji Ashizawa and Torafu Architects.

"I wanted to find a piece of land perched on the cliffs of the caldera, overlooking the volcano and the famous sunsets of Santorini. And when I did, I created a look that mixed minimalistic Cycladic design with a soothing palette of beiges and grays that reflect the eternal feel of the island."

The bold hospitality philosophy of Yannis Bellonias, the Original behind Vora, perfectly captures the singular beauty and spirit of Santorini. At Design Hotels™ we believe in the power of creative expression. That's why each of our 295-plus handpicked independent hotels reflects the ideas of a visionary who is raising the bar on design.

Issue 31

Welcome

The spring issue of *Kinfolk* builds on our foundational interest in design to consider the discipline in its most ambitious manifestation: architecture.

Mid-century architect and furniture designer Charlotte Perriand, whose archives we delve into in this issue, once wrote: "The extension of the art of dwelling is the art of living." We interrogate this close relationship between external surroundings and interior well-being and meet the architects chipping away at the partition wall between the two.

Buildings affect the mood and behavior of their inhabitants. Equally, the things we build—or wish to build—reflect our own state of mind; they're blueprints of the ways in which we hope to reinvent our world. This issue of *Kinfolk* explores the opposing forces that shape our physical environments, paying homage to both the architects with dreams too big for city planners to swallow—as in our investigation into the history of utopian design—and the architects preserving their charming urban fabrics from being swallowed, such as Anne Holtrop and Noura Al Sayeh Holtrop, who are holding on to the heritage of their beloved Bahrain as the Arabian Gulf continues to develop at turbo-speed. We also interview those who have managed to bridge the divide between fact and fiction by making their strangest whims a reality: like Asif Khan, whose belief in a future where architecture is "light, intelligent and simple" inspired him to build with bubbles, and Richard England, whose Maltese monuments to postmodernism we explore in one of our fashion shoots.

Elsewhere in the issue, we meet Sharon Van Etten, who talks about why she chose to study psychology while writing her new album, and we spend a day in rehearsals with Kyle Abraham—the choreographer making history at New York City Ballet. Writer Ellie Violet Bramley explores the history of marriage, narrating the changing nature of an institution no longer wedded to the idea that death us do part; composer Ryuichi Sakamoto describes the creativity that comes when considering his own mortality; and palliative care expert BJ Miller proposes a new meditation with which we might all rethink the inevitable.

As the weather becomes warmer, we turn our faces upward—and toward a cheerier outlook for spring; this issue's essays also find our writers lingering on balconies, musing on the contradictions of "turning over a new leaf" and biting into the juicy mythology of the peach.

JOHN CLIFFORD BURNS & HARRIET FITCH LITTLE

"Music comes after desperation. That happened to me."
RYUICHI SAKAMOTO – P.81

Photograph: Christopher Ferguson

Architecture

"Architects with utopian ambitions don't make easy homes to live in."
LESLIE WILLIAMSON – P.149

Directory

Photography: Romain Laprade

LOEFFLER RANDALL

LOEFFLERRANDALL.COM

45 CHAIR [1945]
BY **FINN JUHL**

www.finnjuhl.com / info@finnjuhl.com / +45 70 277 101

1
Starters

The Newer You

On starting over—and over—again.

"Turning over a new leaf." "Making a fresh start." "Wiping the slate clean." The terms we use to describe big life changes have a sense of intentionality built into them. Nobody would describe being dumped, fired or priced out of a dream home with these words; they are reserved for moments when you've seized power over your behavior and circumstances—when you've made the decision to say goodbye to a bad habit, and feel sure that it will lead to the emergence of a new you.

Often, we make a resolution to visit the gym more and eat differently in the hope of better managing our health; we leave relationships when we feel we have no power to change them and we resign when we're confronted by the prospect of a dead-end job. Moving to another home, city, or even a new country, is often a response to circumstances that we feel are unchangeable and stagnant—a fresh start elsewhere offers the opportunity to begin from scratch and organize things better than before.

We relish the prospect of wholesale change in politics as well as in our personal lives. It's no coincidence that the most familiar refrain from 2016's Brexit referendum campaign in the UK was "take back control," or that Donald Trump struck a chord with supporters when he vowed to "make America great again." Fear and insecurity can prompt a reckless decision to start afresh, no matter the practical implications.

There is an almost spiritual appeal to the notion of the fresh start—with hints of transfiguration, confession and rebirth. Japanese decluttering consultant Marie Kondo's 2011 book *The Life-Changing Magic of Tidying Up* was embraced around the world with almost religious fervor, not because people were looking for nifty solutions to household mess, but because of the implication that disposing of clutter could transform your life. "Identifying what sparks joy leads to a tidy home filled only with items you cherish," Kondo explains on her website. "It's also a path to self-discovery, mindful living and fulfillment."

Yet studies have repeatedly shown that it's difficult to change our fundamental nature. Even lottery winners and those who have experienced life-altering accidents normally revert to their intrinsic state of optimism or pessimism after a short period of time. So why do so many of us remain intoxicated by the notion that we can reinvent ourselves? Not long ago, writer Marianne Power was among this group. After years of feeling vaguely dissatisfied and comparing herself to other people who seemed more productive, successful, healthy and organized, she decided to spend a year making a fresh start every 30 days. "I was seduced by the idea of a new me, who was more positive, organized, productive and rich," she says. "I thought I could fix every flaw I had and, by the end, I'd be a perfect person."

Power's recent book, *Help Me!*, traces her effort to live life according to a different self-help book each month—trying activities ranging from stand-up comedy to approaching men she found attractive on public transportation. She found out soon enough that, if the objective was control, she may never achieve it. "Being human is a messy business—we don't just get to clean it all up, and I think that's often what's driving us: We'd rather not be messy," she says. "There are changes we can make, but I don't think we can ever change the fundamental nature of being human."

It's not that changing your behavior is intrinsically pointless, she says, but it's important to recognize that perfection does not exist. "The main thing I learned was that I didn't really need to change myself—I needed to accept myself and know myself. Now I'm not reading about how to change my life but how to understand it."

She still occasionally gets that familiar feeling of wanting to commit to a new way of being, but now no longer envisages escaping herself. "Turn a new leaf, but also realize your current leaf is fine too—do it, but do it gently."

Photograph: Mon Levchenkova

BJ Miller

"I think my silhouette, the shape of my body, is of comfort to my patients on some level," BJ Miller says. In 1990, the palliative care doctor lost both legs below the knee and his left arm below the elbow when 11,000 volts of electricity shot through his body after he scaled a commuter train with some friends. Miller is now a celebrity of sorts, applauded for the innovative approach to palliative care he took at the Zen Hospice in San Francisco. This July, Miller will publish a book (co-written with Shoshana Berger) titled *A Beginner's Guide to the End*. Talking to *Ben Shattuck*, he explains why we must rethink our approach to the inevitable.

The work you do is very personal—helping people face suffering and their own mortality. Has it been difficult to talk about that so publicly? No question, it has been an unnatural fit and has done funny things to me inside. But I so believe in what we're talking about. My favorite thing about this subject is that it's entirely inclusive. No one is left out. Literally. Whatever fear or discomfort is in me is generally overridden by a feeling of what society needs these days.

Have we lost our way in thinking about death? I think one of the ways death has gotten so hard is that we've been on a steady flight from nature for 170 years or so. Mortality is an enormous, essential fulcrum of nature, and if you see people dying, people suffering, it's hard to seduce yourself into thinking that those things don't exist, that badness doesn't happen. Family dynamics have changed so now you're not living with generations of people—you're not seeing siblings die in childbirth, or living with your dying grandmother. We've disconnected ourselves from that proof of nature within our own families. Instead of relatives helping care for each other, we now ask hospitals to do that—and we need to quit asking medicine to solve everything.

How are you trying to change palliative care? The point of health care is to help people suffer less and to delight in life more, which is also the basic goal of palliative care. One of the problems is that you get all this aggressive care, even hurtful, very expensive care, and then when it's not working or someone's about to die, they say, "Oh, let's do palliative care now." By then, it's too late to reap the benefits. Ideally, palliative care moves further upstream, is present any time a patient or family member is suffering. I'd hope palliative care and health care merge seamlessly so that all health care is infused with palliative care.

A big part of your job is having difficult conversations about death and grieving. Has it given you perspective on your own life? The best goal I have in my own life, taught to me by patients, is, in a nutshell, to appreciate what I have while I still have it. That's the trick. Often, we only let ourselves bask in the fullness of loving someone or something right when it's about to go or has gone. Death is exactly what makes life precious. Period. End of story. But I've learned that I don't have to be on the brink of losing something to appreciate it.

How would you advise people who aren't your patients to prepare for the end? When we mention all the things one can do to prepare for death, their own or someone they love, I fear that we set people up to believe that there are right and wrong ways to do death. People have been dying for a long time, and with each of us there is a relationship with death already. It's in our bones. You know a lot more than you probably think you do about death. You don't have to adopt a bunch of new skills to prepare. There's some of that. But really, mostly, take a huge look inward, and explore from there. In other words: Dear reader, don't worry. You're not going to fail at this.

"I fear that we set people up to believe that there are right and wrong ways to do death."

ELISE BELL

Consider the Peach

Cutting through the mythology of a flirtatious fruit.

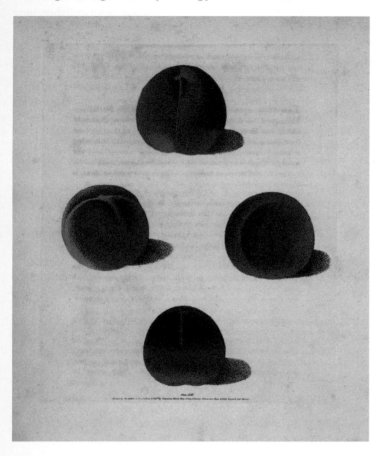

In Caravaggio's *Boy with a Basket of Fruit* (c.1593), peaches evoke sensual possibility: The hot rose blush of the fruits' skin is mirrored in the boy's flushed cheeks. Peaches as a synonym for blossoming lust are also seen in Jan van Eyck's *Arnolfini Portrait* (c.1434), where the impending reality of the newlyweds' bedchamber is suggested by peaches hidden in the corner of the painting. As in 15th-century art history, so in 21st-century popular imagery: From the sticky way peach juice can slip down a chin to the peach-shaped emoji, it is a fruit that continues to capture our erotic imaginations.

Why does the *prunus persica* entice us more than other fruit? Along with its strokeable soft pelt, it helps that the biological structure of the peach aligns itself so closely with the curves of a pert behind—so much so that in 2014, a fruit vendor in Nanjing, China, decided to sell his peaches by dressing them in small satin panties. Patenting his innovation, he called them "Ripe Fruit."

The peach has transcended its role atop the fruit bowl to become pop cultural code. In Selena Gomez's music video for *Fetish ft. Gucci Mane*, the peach is as much a signifier for awakened sexuality as is the plucked wild strawberry of Thomas Hardy's *Tess of the D'Urbervilles*. "I can't deny / your appetite" mouths Gomez into the lascivious gaze of the camera, as she writhes inside a walk-in freezer full of frozen peaches. If *Fetish* is about savage and unruly need, the frozen peaches suggest something previously unawakened; the aching force of young female desire locked in and ready to be devoured.

But to associate the peach solely with feminine sexuality would be to its detriment. A peach knows no such boundaries as gender or sexual orientation; instead it trickles through every layer of popular culture, through cracks and crevices of history. It wends its way from Greek mythology—the peach being the sacred fruit of Hymen, the Greek god of marriage ceremonies—through to the 94th minute of Luca Guadagnino's *Call Me by Your Name*. As Elio rolls his eyes in ecstasy, the complete and rapturous history of the peach is laid bare.

HOT FUZZ
by Harriet Fitch Little

Have you ever told a newborn's parents that their child is so cute you could eat it, or a puppy's owner that it's so fluffy you want to "squeeze it to death"? According to psychologists, it's not a coincidence that so many of the ways we express affection evoke the (hypothetical) desire to hurt things. Known as "cute aggression," the phenomenon is believed to be a way of regulating the excesses of positive emotion we feel when confronted with something particularly adorable. So, people who feel the urge to nibble babies' toes are also more likely to cry at the happiest moment of a film or laugh when something bad happens. Before letting yourself near a puppy, practice regulating your emotions with these inanimate sources of fluff-covered joy. (Top: Charcoal mohair throw by Harlow Henry. Center: Little Petra lounge chair by &tradition. Bottom: Suvé Naderu Brush by Shaquda.)

You don't know what you don't know.

ASHER ROSS
Word: Scienceblind

Etymology: The term was coined by cognitive developmental psychologist Andrew Shtulman as the title for his 2017 book *Scienceblind: Why Our Intuitive Theories About the World Are So Often Wrong.*

Meaning: It's no easy thing to understand the world around us as it really is. We may think we know what causes rainbows, or the seasons, but when asked to explain, our supposedly scientific knowledge can evaporate. In the heat of the moment, we usually revert to intuitive theories.

Heat is a good example. Taking a bath on a winter's day, we might imagine heat as a substance that is "escaping" from the tub. Those with a smattering of physics might think warmer molecules are flowing out of the water, while colder molecules from the air are flooding in. While these intuitive theories of heat transfer are wrong (see radiation, conduction, convection), they work well enough for estimating how long our bath will stay warm, just as they did for our ancestors, huddled around a fire.

Intuitive theories are a normal, even universal part of human cognition. At the societal level, however, they can be quite dangerous. Those who oppose vaccines or GMOs, for example, often have flawed intuitive notions about what is "natural." Shtulman's book is to be read like a catalog of errors that shows just how saturated our minds are, and always have been, by intuitive mistakes.

"It would be easier if there were just a few systemic, general biases that people held, [but] it's not that simple," Shtulman says. Instead, we face the more difficult task of methodically replacing our intuitive theories with scientific knowledge, like the boat that is repaired plank-by-plank at sea. There is no eureka moment in which, as individuals or as a society, we finally achieve a rational worldview.

"These intuitive theories may be with us forever because children will continually reconstruct them from one generation to the next," Shtulman says, noting that even accomplished scientists make intuitive errors outside their own disciplines. "The best option is to have intellectual humility... the recognition that our intuition might always be wrong."

We can be forgiven if we are fond of our private intuitions, like misheard lyrics in a beloved song. The trick is to see them for what they are, and to never hold onto them so tightly that we become blind to reality.

THE END OF THE TUNNEL

by Pip Usher

When an optometrist talks of tunnel vision, they're referring to a loss of peripheral sight. The same applies to a psychological outlook: A person who is suffering from tunnel vision cannot see the full breadth of possibilities because their outlook has become so narrow. Such a condition can be triggered by a scarcity mindset, in which there's a constant fear that there simply isn't enough—whether that be food, finances or emotional fulfillment. Obsessed with alleviating this perceived shortage, a scarcity mindset will respond with short-term, impulse-led behaviors. As a result, the ability to consider long-term priorities, and the joy of creatively strategizing on how to get there, is replaced by an obsessive drive to meet immediate needs and desires. Avoid falling into this trap by regularly exercising original thinking and opening the mind to new possibilities. A useful metaphor can be found in The Alternative Uses Test, designed in 1967, which challenges participants to come up with as many uses as possible for a simple object like a paper clip. Could it be fashioned into a hair clip? Reimagined as a zipper? Take two minutes to jot ideas down and then match your results against the test's four-part metric system. At first, you may find it tricky to shake that dogged fixation on the object's paper-organizing purposes; that's tunnel vision. But keep practicing and soon a world of possibility will emerge.
Photography by Lorenz Kienzle

The *Girl* director discusses the language of dance.

SALA ELISE PATTERSON

Lukas Dhont

"Overwhelming." That's how Belgian film director Lukas Dhont describes debuting his first feature film, *Girl*, at the 2018 Cannes Film Festival and walking away with four prizes. Although only 27 years old, Dhont has already established a reputation as a deft teller of interior stories that take root within one person but make emotional sense to all. The film probes the adolescent world of an ambitious transgender ballet dancer, Lara, played by Victor Polster. Dhont brings us achingly close to it all— Lara's obsession with becoming a prima ballerina and the struggle to feel at home in the body she relies on to do it.

How would you describe your approach to filmmaking? I went to a film school that combines documentary and fiction, so I make fiction films but with a documentary influence. For example, *Girl* is based on a story that I read in the newspaper in 2009 about a young transgender dancer named Nora.

Dance also played a role in your earlier short films. Why? As a young boy I danced and even though I quit very early, I still have this enormous passion for dance and people who use their bodies to communicate or make art. I also have an interest in physicality because for 21 years I didn't really allow myself to get into an intimate physical relationship with someone. So, in my work, I always try— literally—to touch people. That's why my cameras are very close and near to the skin.

So dance has become part of your cinematic language? Yes. I don't think it always has to be in a literal way. It could also be in the way that we use the camera as a choreographer around movement or actors. I'm interested in this form of storytelling. I think my films will always focus more on the visual than on the spoken word.

What parts of Nora's story did you fictionalize and why? Nora's story has a very classic hero/villain structure, in which someone wants to fight the outside world to be accepted. At first, we wrote that version of the script. But we found that the film was much more about the outside world than it was about this trans character. We really wanted to focus on her and not on the negativity around her.

What does Nora think? Oh, she loves it. She is our biggest fan.

Photograph: Frederik Vercruysse, Location: Fosbury & Sons, Boitsfort

ERIK
jørgensen
THE MANUFACTURER

OVO – The perfect balance

Ovo is a refined easy chair, designed by Damian Williamson, with striking curves resting on a rigid squared steel frame. The same steel is also used as a beautiful slim line connecting the back and the front of the chair. As a result, you achieve a playful integration between the leather and the steel while hiding the stitched seam at the same time.

The Ovo design is first and foremost about generosity but also great comfort. The chair is welcoming and very comfortable to sit in – it invites you to sit back and relax. Whether you place it in the comfort of your own private home, a relaxing hotel suite or a lobby, it will be the perfect fit.

WWW.ERIK-JOERGENSEN.COM

How to Gossip

In *The Gossips*, one of American painter Norman Rockwell's most amusing and cartoonish works, he follows a tidbit of gossip as it passes from person to person until it finally reaches the ears of the subject of the rumor. He confronts the original tattletale—who is shocked that her indiscreet whisper has traveled back to its source.

Most of us yield to the temptation, at least occasionally, to relay a story that would be better kept untold. It doesn't feel quite right, but we tell the tale anyway. So why do we do it? While we know that it can inflict real harm on a person's reputation, it can also enhance our own. Gossip reinforces connections to influential people and puts us in the information loop; huddling together with sympathetic listeners might protect us later on.

In fact, in a recent study of workplace gossip, a team of psychologists from the University of Waterloo in Canada, led by Daniel Brady, showed that, far from being a deviant practice, gossip serves a positive role in building group cohesion. They explain that gossip conveys "information regarding what it means to be a member of the group, thereby enabling the construction of group identity." They also point out that, for individuals, gossip "capitalizes on norms of reciprocity"—it builds mutual trust; it also helps clarify ways to function successfully in the group. Other researchers have echoed these findings: Despite the immediate pain it might inflict, gossip is a beneficial social practice.

These surprisingly positive accounts of gossip are not all good news for malicious conductors of compromising information, however. Researchers point out that most people think badly about gossip because they associate it with mean behavior. They don't realize that most gossip falls under the broad, rather benign definition of "evaluative talk about a person who is not present."

When the subject of whispers eventually hears them, is there a remedy or a way for everyone to move on with their reputation intact? Almost certainly, as long as the intent doesn't feel spiteful—and the item of gossip hasn't acquired an unpleasant new shape through its repeated tellings.

Gossips usually trade mild judgment of relatively minor concerns—those judgments might even be positive. When things turn negative, as they naturally do sometimes, gossip can still be useful as long as it serves collective goals and avoids malice. Perhaps sharing someone else's error can even steer listeners away from making similar lapses. For the same reason, malicious rumormongers always deserve to be talked about behind their backs.

According to behavioral scientist Kevin Kniffin, groups generally engage in malicious gossip only when the subject of the gossip is perceived to be slacking.

Photograph: Courtesy of Verner Panton Design

Photograph: Claire Benoist / The Licensing Project

Actors are notorious for spoiling their own movies. David Prowse accidentally revealed that Darth Vader was Luke Skywalker's father two years before the release of *The Empire Strikes Back*.

You might remember where you were on July 19, 2007. In New York City, it was sunny and cool, with a scattering of popcorn clouds sweeping overhead. Most importantly, it was a Thursday—two days before the official release of the final Harry Potter book. And yet, on every newsstand that morning was a *New York Times* book review titled, "An Epic Showdown as Harry Potter Is Initiated Into Adulthood."

By the fifth paragraph, readers were told, among other spoilers, that half a dozen beloved characters died, that a war had begun, that Voldemort's followers breached the walls of Hogwarts and that Harry and Voldemort fought.

Anger flooded the internet. J.K. Rowling said she was "staggered that some American newspapers would publish purported spoilers in the form of reviews in complete disregard of the wishes of literally millions of readers, particularly children." The *New York Post* responded with the article, "Why Does N.Y. Times Hate Kids."

We don't like spoilers. Or, as it turns out, we *think* we don't like spoilers. A 2011 study from UC San Diego proved that we enjoy a story more—not less—if we know the ending. College students given full synopses of stories (including their surprise endings) reported greater satisfaction (on a scale of one to 10) after reading than students given the same stories without synopses. "Spoilers are actually story enhancers," one researcher said. "You get to see this broader view, and essentially understand the story more fluently."

But the angry resistance is real. (Try convincing a *Game of Thrones* fan that empirical evidence shows it's better to know ahead of time who dies by the end of each season.) Where that feeling comes from is a question the researchers didn't ask, but it's one that's worth considering.

In a story, you travel beside a character, binding your consciousness to theirs. You build intimacy through empathy—experiencing the world as he or she does, coming to resolution together. If you already knew that Jane Eyre was falling in love with a married man, you wouldn't feel her same swoop of devastation on her wedding day and, when she later discovers him widowed, the swell of joy the moment she touches his outstretched hand. Knowing the ending would mean a break from Jane's reality—a step away from her intimate purview and toward the author's overview instead. When a story is spoiled, you lose that wild openness that you might feel in your own life—surprise coming without warning and changing you in ways you can't imagine. That unfolding sense of mystery can't be measured in a laboratory on a one-to-10 scale of satisfaction.

"You lose that wild openness you might feel in your own life."

ASHER ROSS

Can It

Is it possible to laugh alone? There are certainly times when we burst out laughing all by ourselves. But usually, we think of laughter as a group activity.

In the classic *Laughter: An Essay on the Meaning of the Comic*, Henri Bergson wrote, "However spontaneous it seems, laughter always implies a kind of secret freemasonry, or even complicity, with other laughers, real or imaginary." To laugh alone is to remember the social atmosphere of past laughter: the giddiness over cocktails, the scrunched-up face of the curmudgeonly aunt.

For most of human history, entertainment was a public affair, and theatergoers experienced comedy as a crowd. This was also true of cinema. When the Marx Brothers started making movies in the 1930s, they could be sure that laughter would roll through the movie theater just as naturally as it had when they performed in vaudeville. But television produced a novel problem that made executives nervous: Would people still laugh if they couldn't hear the crowd?

The fix came from American sound engineer Charles Douglass, who in the 1950s created his notorious "laff box," a rudimentary sampler that could add prerecorded laughter to edited shows. With it, producers developed a sonic progression that can be heard on sitcoms through the decades, from *The Andy Griffith Show* to *Seinfeld* to *Friends*: soft murmurs, then chortles and, when the big gag comes, implausible belly laughs.

Yet between the late 1980s and the early aughts, there was a backlash. If one had to choose a turning point, it might be the original British version of *The Office*, which ushered in a new, darker style of comedy that replaced canned laughter with awkward, pregnant silence.

By now this comic style is de rigueur, leaving the laugh track to become glaringly uncool (though it lives on in a handful of mainstream sitcoms). It seems unlikely that this is because laughter no longer needs company. Instead, company has become so ubiquitous that we no longer need the cue. Social media can make us feel like we are always in the presence of like-minded strangers—a collective chorus of feedback that never fully subsides. To put it another way, we are never without Bergson's "imaginary" audience.

In our digital worlds, we tend to get angry together, express irony together and whine together. Most pleasantly, we laugh together. To hear the canned version now feels annoyingly superfluous. We used to laugh along with the laff box. Now we mock it. There's no getting rid of that "we" though, it would seem.

Photograph: Gustav Almestål, Set Designer: Matilda Beckman

HEAR, HEAR!

by Harriet Fitch Little

The world's loudest speaker system would be an unwelcome addition to any living room. Located in the Netherlands, the Large European Acoustic Facility (LEAF, for short) can produce noises equivalent to that of four jets taking off simultaneously. Rather than blasting out tunes at the scientists' Christmas party, it's used to test the ability of rocket parts to withstand the sonic impact of take-off. No one's quite sure what effect hearing it would produce (the giant horns are secluded behind steel- and rubber-coated walls.) Most likely, the listener's ear drums would break, and their internal organs rupture. Better play it safe, and opt for one of these stylish, organ-friendly alternatives. (Top: Beoplay P6 by Bang & Olufsen. Center: Portable radio in Cognac by Geneva. Bottom: Portable Bluetooth Tube Audio Speaker by LEFF Amsterdam.)

Right Photograph: Benoit Paillé, Left Photography: Bang & Olufsen, goodhoodstore.com, WallpaperSTORE*

CHARLES SHAFAIEH

Semi-detached

Unease in suburbia.

The opening scene of David Lynch's 1986 film *Blue Velvet* begins as a snapshot of the beatific suburban life to which many aspire—until the camera pushes deep underneath the well-manicured lawn and reveals a foundation of violence and mess, as beetles and other insects collide in the dirt. This chaotic display suggests that the above-ground trappings of the "suburban dream"—from white picket fences to the pristine homes they enclose—are no less disturbing.

Suburbia hasn't always been treated with such suspicion. Historian Kenneth T. Jackson argued that the growth of suburban settlements—city-adjacent residential neighborhoods built with commuters in mind—was intended to create a new sense of self and family. "The new ideal was no longer to be part of a close community, but to have a self-contained unit, a private wonderland walled off from the rest of the world," he wrote in *Crabgrass Frontier*, his 1985 study of America's suburban sprawl. The threats are merely different in suburbia, however, and the sense of privacy and freedom an illusion. Behavior is controlled and order maintained because residents know they are always being watched by their neighbors. Is the grass too long? Are the teenagers outside smoking? Does the house need to be repainted? Like in Jeremy Bentham's panopticon, suburbanites have internalized the idea that *someone* is watching them. Street-facing picture windows are designed to showcase the life within, but in many developments, residents need never look inside a neighbor's house to know the floor plan. When only a few house designs were offered in the subdivision, their kitchen may be just like everyone else's.

Both within and across such developments, this repetitive, limited architecture creates no-places which are separated from the rest of society except by car. At night, these cookie-cutter designs suggest that there is nothing about them worthy of attention, that robbers or other disturbances should just pass them by. But as Lynch's film reveals, it is the strange nature of their drabness that in part elicits the disquieting thoughts that suburbia wants suppressed.

Asif Khan

Photography: Matthew Attard Navarro

"Temporary projects are opportunities to develop manifestos."

The future of London is taking shape in the studio of Asif Khan. The architect is hard at work on an imaginative new Museum of London building that will combine the city's history with its contemporary creativity. At 39, he's one of the youngest architects to design such a major cultural institution in recent memory. It's a "dream project" for Khan, who has spent the last 10 years building his reputation with temporary architecture like walk-through pavilions and tech-heavy installations.

Along the way, the born-and-bred South Londoner and father of two has picked up awards as varied as a Cannes Lions from the advertising industry and an MBE from the British royal family. A recent structure at the Winter Olympics was coated in the world's blackest black, to dizzying effect. Other projects interrupt the urban environment with forest-like oases, offering calm. "I want to connect people better with their own nature," he says.

Why is temporary architecture important? It's very common for architects, and it always has been, to start with temporary architec-ture. They're the only projects that regularly get offered to architects who are starting out. At the same time, they're experimental projects where you're using technology in new ways. They're opportunities to develop manifestos. What happens is, those ideas that we test through temporary buildings, exhibition designs or installations, weave their way into the permanent projects we do.

What about something really esoteric, like the installation you did with soap bubbles (*In the Clouds*, 2011)—*has* that cropped up later as something practical? The cloud project directly informs a building we're working on now in Kazakhstan [the Tselinny Center of Contemporary Culture in Almaty]. We've done two or three projects, maybe more, incorporating the idea of clouds—it keeps coming up. And it's really about creating diffuse, lightweight, translucent volumes.

Is there a common motivation underlying everything that you do as an architect? Whether we're making something with timber or stone or glass or some kind of dig-ital medium, it's always about trying to connect with the individual and their senses. Think of the experiences we have in nature: breathing in the air on top of a mountain, stepping through snow, feeling sunlight on our face, diving into an ocean and almost getting vertigo from looking down at the seabed. I want architecture to inspire those feelings.

You're currently working on your biggest project to date, the Museum of London, with Stanton Williams. What should people expect when they enter it? One of our tasks is to let people experience a building [the Victorian-era Smithfield market] that's been lost from London's memory, let them feel the stories that have happened there over the last 150 years—the patina, the surfaces, the smells, the light quality. At the same time, people will experience a new type of museum that isn't just about objects, it's about the generation of new ideas. It will host a variety of partner institutions that are collaborating and creating new content and challenging the city to think about itself in a new way. It will be the place where the conversations about the future of London happen.

A number of your works have been spaces to meditate or find calm. Is meditation something that you practice yourself? I've explored a little bit; I'd like to go further with it. I run. I find that allows you to switch off certain thoughts and be in a void of some sort.

Did you design the home you live in? I did with a previous home. The current one is an as-found, Victorian, inappropriate, fall-down-the-stairs kind of house.

What have you aimed to create for yourself in those living spaces? I want the space to be capable of supporting various levels of relaxation and attentiveness, the full range. So you can have a serious meeting with someone, you can recline whilst reading a book, you can get on one elbow after you've had a bath and enjoy the heat, and you can lie down fully and take a nap, or sleep there overnight and not feel bad about it. It's not about multifunctionality; it's about the room being able to comfort you no matter what time of day it is.

CHARLES SHAFAIEH

On the Balcony

A view from the inside out.

Balconies are transitional spaces—at once inside and outside, private and public. They are also a luxury: However pleasant they may be for lounging or useful for circulating air through apartments in hot climates, they cannot be considered essential.

These semi-enclosed spaces create illusions. Balcony-dwellers are seen but not heard, among the people but separate—and even protected—from them, as monarchs and presidents know well. Balconies trick an audience gathered for royal wedding celebrations or a pope's speech into believing, if only for a moment, that strict social hierarchies do not exist since everyone is sharing the same air. But the very nature of the balcony's design—that it cannot be put on the ground floor—reinforces the notion that its inhabitants are meant to be, both literally and figuratively, above the rest.

The effect a simple balcony can have, for leader and follower alike, was well understood by the architects who submitted a proposal in the early 1930s for the Palazzo del Littorio, Rome's future Fascist Party headquarters. They wrote about what the inclusion of a balcony would bring to the design: "[Mussolini] is like a God, outlined against the sky; above Him there is no one… The Duce will stand before adoring multitudes; He will belong to everyone, He will be one with everyone." Mussolini himself clearly grasped the power this architectural feature could conjure: He chose to declare war on France and Britain, and to proclaim Italy an empire, from the balcony of the Palazzo Venezia. The spot became so symbolically associated with him that it was closed for years following the war.

Less sinister is the long-held association between balconies and amorous desire. Although Shakespeare never mentioned a balcony in *Romeo and Juliet*, it is ubiquitous in stagings of the play. The balcony is a physical site where Juliet can move closer to her lover while still remaining inside her father's house. In this, she is not alone. For women largely confined to interiors, balconies afford opportunities to "leave" the home without exiting the front door, complete with a stage that allows them to both look outward and display themselves.

That one of the most famous paintings with a balcony, Manet's *The Balcony*, features women is therefore unsurprising. What seems peculiar, however, is that neither of the two women depicted in the foreground appear to be looking at anything at all. Instead, their deadened stares suggest pure introspection—self-voyeurism that subverts popular connotations of the balcony as a site of degenerate exhibitionism. Magritte considered these women to be far from liberated: In his *Perspective: Manet's Balcony*, he copies Manet's painting but puts nailed-up coffins where the people should be. A balcony may satisfy a voyeuristic impulse as its occupant gazes into others' apartments or examines a neighbor's private life through their laundry as it hangs drying. Both Manet and Magritte suggest, however, that they remain a world apart—on balconies, people are caged-in in ways that go beyond the railings that surround them.

Balconies allow public figures to be seen but not touched. In the UK, Buckingham Palace's sweeping Royal Balcony has long been a focal point for national celebrations.

Photograph: Romain Laprade

Photography: Claire Cottrell

Meet the sculptor who wrings succulence from stone.

ELISE BELL

Nevine Mahmoud

Even prior to working with stone, Mahmoud was preoccupied with materiality and exploring "the reasons why certain things make you want to touch them."

Nevine Mahmoud is ill, which means she's enjoying a moment of rest. "I'm not very good at taking breaks," she says. "I'd been feeling like I was getting sick for a while but I was ignoring the signs. The studio is my home, you know." But Mahmoud's Los Angeles studio is no ordinary studio, no ordinary home: It's outdoors, and full of tools more associated with a mason's yard than an artist's loft. Mahmoud—who trained in London before flying west to pursue her studies at the University of Southern California—makes larger-than-life carvings that juxtapose the softness of flesh with the solidity of stone. Her work is gaining recognition following her triumphant 2018 solo show, *Foreplay*.

What in everyday life do you find the most sensual? There are a lot of tactile things about being with another person, but really in terms of the everyday it's being in certain buildings, where the material is all around you and totally encompassing you. It can feel so theatrical, almost as if you are role-playing in a set, and that can be so thrilling and sensual. I was actually in a new architectural environment in China and staying in this hotel that was so moody and dark, with concrete everywhere.

It doesn't need to be luxurious, but an attention to the materials all around you and being very direct with the materials you use is so common in architecture and that's why I find so much joy in it. My respect for artistic materials very much transitions to buildings. I built my own house and my own studio.

Your work deals a lot in attraction. When did you find yourself attracted to stone? For me, coming to LA was partly about this weird cultural climate that was so exotic [compared to] the history of England. I knew from the outset that the materials here were so much more accessible; I could walk into a metal workshop if I wanted to, or walk into a quarry. I started to get to know people outside of my art class and I would go photograph their studios which were outdoor studio complexes. I became fascinated by people who worked in stone and wanted to know more about their method and craft. One day I brought this big stone into class and said to my professor, "I can't be bothered to do this school trip. Can I just go and learn stone carving instead?" I could never shake off the feeling that I just needed to do it. After grad school I went back to the idea of stone,

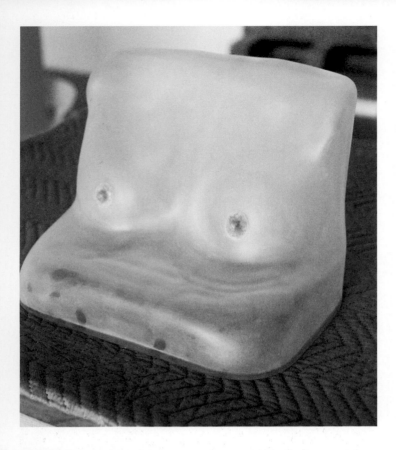

really latching onto the fact that I wanted a teacher. So when I got my mentor, I saw this beautiful, big orange rock and I knew I had to come up with something quick, an idea to pin my learning onto. I was like: "What if I made this into a peach?"

In your 2018 solo exhibition, *Foreplay,* **there is an abundance of sensual imagery related to fruit. Why is that?** The fruit came with the stonework in a way. I wanted to work with a traditional material and sync it up with myself and my perspective as a woman. My thought process became: "What would be the most interesting way to undermine the materiality of stone, which is hard and resistant and not edible? What would be the inverse of that?" [It was a] contrast I was immediately drawn to, especially as these oversized objects take on the size and scale of a body part: A torso-sized peach—do you want to eat it?

What work of art do you wish you had made? It changes every two years, but [the Polish sculptor] Alina Szapocznikow inspired me to look at my work more personally and be more forward with my sensual and sexual desires. Her resin lip lamp and all those variations of her body and her face in resin and bronze, those are just perfect to me. I'm not good at being too quick and crafty, but the beauty

and the looseness of her work continue to excite me.

Do you find stone carving to be relaxing? I've always worked in a very industrious way that's required a lot of mental and physical focus. For me, I need my process to be labor-intensive or my head spins out. The more physical it is, the more meditative it is.

You relocated to LA because the materials attracted you. Are there any other places where you feel you could be inspired? I'm not sure about how long I'll be in LA for. I'm old enough now to enjoy the security of staying in one place, but I'm not stuck here forever. I don't think I could ever consider not working outdoors. It's good for your health; it's good for you mentally. According to the stone carvers here, Santiago in Chile is a great place to carve due to its proximity to Argentina and the mines there.

Should we expect to see an evolution between *Foreplay* **and the work you're creating now?** I think I'll always be making large, sensual work, but the material will change. I have a habit of moving on to a different material every three years. I don't agree with sticking with one motif for the sake of having a motif. *Foreplay* certainly was a great playground for me to try out stone and create a lasting stamp

for my experience with that material, but I've since found myself working with glass. It's the supple nature and how it looks like liquid that I've become really drawn to, especially in a figurative sense: How you can make glass look like breasts, for example.

It's an interesting move: Stone is so hard and durable, whereas glass is delicate. I know. Again it's a paradox, how something as fragile as glass can also be so resistant and strong. The tools you can use for glass are the same in terms of heaviness and physicality as the utensils for stone.

A lot of female artists often feel the need to justify their figurative work by instilling a feminist message. Is there a reason why you are returning to the human body, particularly the female body? I'm interested in displaced, broken up body parts, but really a lot of it comes down to myself and my own fascination and obsession with women's breasts and how they are so prevalent and objectified. I think I spent a long time shying away from figurative objects and trying to find figures in inanimate, abstracted work. It's been very productive for me, having these moments of inserting actual renderings of the body to scale. I'm enjoying working with them and I love how fucking weird they look.

"Architecture is very sexy to me," says Mahmoud. "Spaces can feel very theatrical, almost as if you are role-playing in a set."

2
Features

FV

For a decade, French painter *Fabienne Verdier* lived in China and studied under the few calligraphy masters who

survived the Cultural Revolution. Then she came home to Paris, and applied their teachings on an epic scale.

Words by *Daphnée Denis* & Photography by *Jean-Marie Franceschi*

"My transgression was to understand that I had to cut off the handle of my brush."

A few years ago, Fabienne Verdier dislocated her shoulder trying to carry a paintbrush so heavy she couldn't move it around without hurting herself. "It was because of all my crazy experiments, I didn't pay enough attention," she says with a mischievous giggle.

What kind of paintbrush can put a shoulder out? Verdier invented it. The 57-year-old artist, who spent 10 years learning the art of calligraphy from old masters in China, works with an unusual set of oversized devices inspired by the traditional Chinese brush. They are giant, handleless brushes made from up to 25 horsetails and capable of holding over 25 gallons of paint. Verdier suspends them from the ceiling of her studio in Le Vexin, an hour north of Paris, and maneuvers them with bicycle handlebars mounted onto the ferrule of each brush. Every painting is the result of a spontaneous choreography performed as a pas de deux with one of her signature tools over carefully prepared canvases spread across the floor.

Still, when she hurt her shoulder, the bike handlebars proved useless. Her brushes were too heavy to handle with just one arm. So she had to come up with a new system while she healed: what she calls "walking paintings." "I totally dematerialized the Chinese brush, and created a funnel, kind of like a witch's hat, where I put my materials... and I modulate it like a musician traversing space," says (a fully recovered) Verdier, mimicking the gesture. She is sitting at the Galerie Lelong & Co., in the eighth arrondissement of Paris, where she is showing her series of paintings *Ainsi la Nuit* ("Thus the Night") for the first time. The exhibition, named after a string quartet by contemporary composer Henri Dutilleux, presents both brush works and "night walks"—streams of black paint poured over dark blue panels inspired by the changing colors of the night. The largest piece—a 13-foot-long triptych—sells for $240,000.

Since she returned to France in 1993, Verdier has become quite the sensation in the art world. Her work blends the Western influences of abstract expressionists like Mark Rothko with the philosophy and traditional craft she studied under master calligraphers and painters in China. She's written a critically acclaimed memoir of her apprenticeship there, presented solo exhibitions across Europe and Asia and sold paintings to prestigious collections—the Centre Pompidou in Paris, the Pinakothek der Moderne in Munich, the Juilliard School in New York. Last year, she was commissioned to create the poster for the French Open tennis tournament. The year before, the iconic French dictionary Petit Robert asked Verdier to produce a series of paintings to celebrate their 50th anniversary. She's come a long way, literally. At age 22, freshly graduated from the École des Beaux-Arts in Toulouse, Verdier obtained a scholarship to pursue her studies at the Sichuan Fine Arts Institute, a communist-led art school in the city of Chongqing. Fascinated by traditional landscape paintings, she'd set out to learn from the old masters who still lived in the province. In the early 1980s, this was a risky endeavor. Mao Zedong's Cultural Revolution, a youth-led purge against the country's intellectual elites, had ravaged China's cultural landscape less than a decade earlier. The scholars who had survived hid away in retirement, banned from passing on the secrets of their craft.

"It was a great, great tragedy," Verdier says with a long sigh. "It took me a lot of time to find the last old scholars who hadn't been rehabilitated. And they were afraid to teach me anything at all because I was

Hair & Makeup: Claire Plekhoff

Verdier was the first artist-in-residence at Juilliard, where she explored the possibility of translating music into paint.

"Accidents have a way of making us reinvent ourselves," say Verdier, who continues to pioneer new methods to facilitate her painting on an epic scale.

"I was a foreigner, and a woman on top of that."

a foreigner, and because I was a woman on top of that... There were no women who practiced that form of art."

After meeting master Huang Yuan, the man who would eventually initiate her into the art of calligraphy, Verdier spent months trying to convince him she was worth the trouble. Every day, she would copy ideograms from secondhand books and drop them at his door, while her classmates mocked her bizarre obsession.

Tall and slender, with light brown hair and piercing green eyes, the French apprentice must have stood out among a crowd of 2,000 Chinese artists-in-training. Yet, in the beginning, none of her classmates spoke to her. The Communist bureau had put up a sign outside her door expressly forbidding any contact with the "foreign student." "I lived in frightful solitude," she remembers. The school board expected her to leave in a matter of weeks. Verdier stayed.

Once she was able to decipher the message at her door, she demanded to be treated like everyone else. To fight loneliness, she got herself a pet myna bird, a species known for being able to duplicate human speech—only to find out hers was mainly taught to curse by its previous owners. One day, she heard a soft knock at her door. Before she could answer, the bird invited her guest in with a swift "Enter, you buffoon." It was master Huang Yuan.

"He told me he accepted to transmit his art to me, that he would request special authorizations, because of what he saw in my exercises, in my tenacity," Verdier says. "Then he added that if I wanted to learn, it would be 10 years or nothing. The culture was so complicated, it was the only way it would work. So I accepted... I had no idea what I was getting myself into." She bursts into laughter, her face lighting up at the memory of how it all started.

Until then, Verdier had been quite the unruly student. Back in Toulouse, she would skip class to draw at the Natural History Museum instead. "I thought that the way we were taught to represent things was... it was like a skeleton, it was too rigid," she says. "Our traditions of geometric construction, seeing the world through a vanishing point, the laws of perspective, all of those things trapped us, formatted us in a way that seemed..." She pauses. "It seemed dead." When Huang became her mentor, however, her restlessness was put to the test. For weeks on end, the old master would only let her draw a single line, never quite satisfied with the result. Contrary to the Western method of painting

horizontally on a canvas stretched out on an easel, the art of Chinese brush painting is a vertical affair. The resemblance to the subject matter is of little importance. Brush strokes are meant to flow naturally to capture the "qi," the vital force of what is represented, as perceived by the artist. There can be no mistakes because there are no corrections. Mastering how to trace that one line is key.

Was it trying for a rebellious soul to abide by such strict rules? For Verdier, the transgression of learning ancient traditions in a country that had sought to destroy them felt rebellious enough. "What I was doing was forbidden. Huang had been authorized to teach me, but the other masters I visited hadn't. I had to be very discreet." A picture of her early training shows Verdier leaning over master Cheng Jun, who taught her the art of seal carving. In his right hand, he is holding the small blade he uses for engraving. He has no left hand. It was cut off by revolutionaries so he would stop practicing his art.

Verdier compares her time in China to the years a classically trained musician spends learning to play great composers. "I focused on performing the art of calligraphy, much like a musician learns to perform Bach, Fauré, Mozart... Becoming a good performer is already a creation in and of itself. I was only able to start breaking the rules once I was back in France, when I locked myself in and started to digest everything."

Coming home was a shock. Verdier had only flown back to France once over the course of 10 years. She'd met her husband, Ghislain Baizeau, in China. Together, they moved into a home in the countryside, not far from Paris. That's where she started to work on "creating a new language," a synthesis between her Western influences and what she'd learned in the Sichuan province. She quickly gave up the small Chinese brush and decided to start painting with her whole body. Doing that meant breaking tradition. "My biggest transgression was to understand that I had to cut off the handle of my brush and transplant the handlebars of my bicycle onto it," she says, almost as if she'd had to perform surgery on a human being. "My body, my brain and my brush became one, and suddenly I discovered a third dimension in my brush stroke, you see?" With her index finger, she follows the curves of white paint dancing on one of her canvases, a "living line traversing space."

What she set out to do left many perplexed. "I was very unhappy at first because the Chinese no longer understood me, they didn't get why I didn't remain a great performer of Chinese tradition... And Westerners

thought that since I had been educated by Chinese people, I was only doing *chinoiseries* [European imitations of East-Asian art]." That last critique stung hard. Throughout her apprenticeship, Verdier had made it clear she had no interest in imitation or pretending to be someone else. When master Huang Yuan offered to find her a Chinese name, she refused. "I am not Chinese," she told him. She knew some would question her legitimacy to explore ancient Asian traditions as a Western artist, but, she says, she wanted to "learn to think differently, to think Chinese."

Verdier's art is very much a fusion of both worlds: traditional and modern, spontaneous and meticulously prepared. Like her Chinese masters, she mainly draws inspiration from nature, seeking to grasp "a moment in a brushstroke," rather than "to build a representation of the world through touch-ups," the figurative artists' approach. But that doesn't mean she doesn't also feed off Western schools of thought.

Since 2014, Verdier has been interested in painting the sound of music. She became the first artist-in-residence at Juilliard, in New York, where she set up a "laboratory" with jazz and classical musicians to try and capture the vibrations of music through her brush strokes. She later worked alongside a string quartet at the Visitation Chapel of Aix-en-Provence to compose her series *Ainsi la Nuit*. "I would listen to the music and suddenly, all of the universe I had set up for over 30 years no longer worked. It forced me to step out of my comfort zone. It was very violent, very challenging, but it forced me to find new visual structures I didn't know I had in me," she says.

> "I think that I am, in fact, an adventurer. Leave schools and walls behind, go out and breathe life."

The act of painting itself can be done in a matter of minutes, but each piece represents months of planning. She burns a large part of her production—albeit "a little bit less than [she] used to." "Sometimes, my brush grasps the ideal moment, but a lot of the time, I'm totally off the mark, I become too pretentious, too heavy-handed, too obsessive," says Verdier, sheepishly. "It's difficult to talk about it. A moment of grace is very rare."

So to fight feelings of inadequacy, she religiously keeps *carnets d'atelier*. These are scrapbooks in which she compiles all her research into a given theme: philosophers' quotes, article clippings, photographs, anything that resonates with the energy she wants to portray.

"It's a chaos of thoughts and images…" she says, leafing through her 2017 scrapbook, filled with reflections on her night walks, pictures of constellations and taped reproductions of works of art by Cy Twombly or Sigmar Polke. "When I spend several hours carrying 100 liters of pictorial matter, when I can't get my internal visions out, the only thing that consoles me is to read poets, philosophers… and to find in their writings something that I'm going through myself, the same intuitions."

She who once traveled across continents to seek guidance from foreign masters now seeks to explore something deeper within herself. "I think that I am, in fact, an adventurer," she says in the opening of the documentary *Painting the Moment*, "but not only in the sense of discovering new territories in real life. It's an internal adventure I'm after."

Recently, Verdier has been following in the footsteps of post-impressionist painter Paul Cézanne, making work for the Musée Granet in Aix-en-Provence. Naturally, she invented a new tool with which to do so: a metallic structure capable of carrying her giant brushes out in the open to be able to work in direct contact with nature. One day, as she was sitting on a rock, some young art students came up to see her, she recalls. "They told me they were bored, so I advised them to take their initiatory journey. Leave schools and walls behind, go out and breathe life." She pauses and grins, as if remembering the days when she, too, skipped art school in the South of France.

The Drive

Photography by *Luc Braquet* & Styling by *Camille-Joséphine Teisseire*

Mamadou wears a suit by Samsøe & Samsøe, a rollneck sweater by De Fursac, socks by Falke and a belt and shoes by J.M. Weston. Previous spread: Loane wears a dress by Rochas and a hat by Laurence Bossion.

Top: Loane wears a dress by Dior, a headpiece by Laurence Bossion and earrings by Chanel. Bottom: Mamadou wears a suit, shirt and silk tie by Hermès, a handkerchief by Charvet and shoes by J.M. Weston.

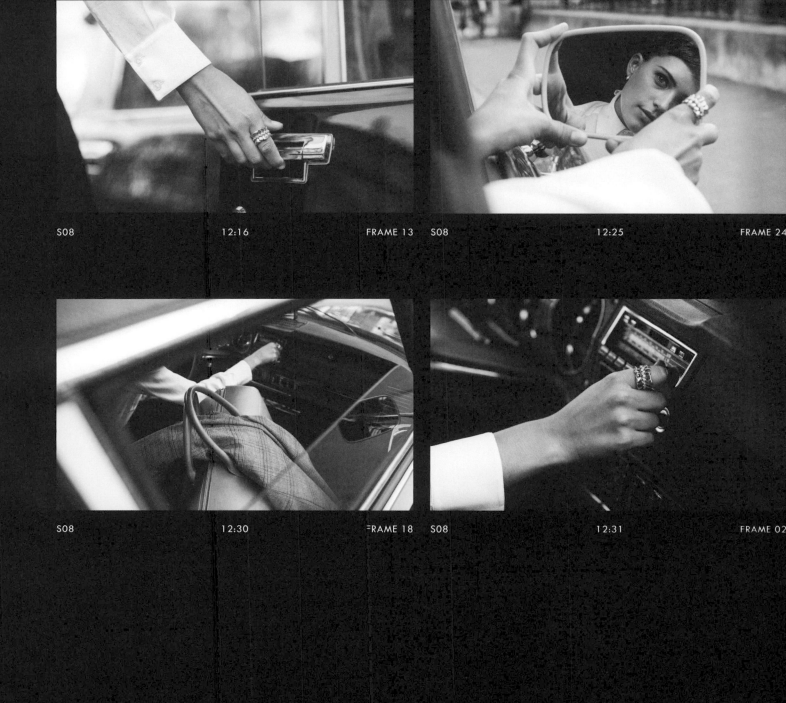

S08   12:16   FRAME 13   S08   12:25   FRAME 24

S08   12:30   FRAME 18   S08   12:31   FRAME 02

Loane wears a top by Rochas, earrings by Yannis Sergakis at White Bird and a ring by Dior. Bag by Mansur Gavriel and jacket by Samsøe & Samsøe.

Mamadou wears a suit by Paul Smith, a shirt by Charvet, a silk tie by Hermès and a cap by Stetson. Loane wears a coat by Dior.

Top: Loane wears a top by COS, a skirt by Dior, a beret by Hermès, shoes by Rochas, earrings by Yannis Sergakis at White Bird and carries a bag by Dior.
Bottom: Loane wears a top by Rochas, a skirt by Dior and a hat by Laurence Bossion. Mamadou wears a coat by De Fursac, a sweater and trousers by Jacquemus, a shirt by Charvet, socks by Falke and a belt and shoes by J.M. Weston.

S14   17:56   FRAME 11   S15   18:33   FRAME 23

S15   18:45   FRAME 02   S15   18:52   FRAME 21

Top left: Loane wears a coat and shoes by Dior, gloves by Causse, stockings by Saint Laurent, and carries a bag by Edie Parker. Mamadou wears a suit by Paul Smith, a shirt by Charvet, silk tie by Hermès, a cap by Stetson, socks by Falke and shoes by J.M. Weston. See Credits on page 191 for further details.

Top: Mamadou wears a coat by 3.1 Phillip Lim and a shirt by Hermès. Loane wears a dress by Mugler, hat by Laurence Bossion and earrings by Chanel.
Bottom: Loane wears a dress by Dior and the same accessories.

S16   21:02   FRAME 12

S16   21:27   FRAME 19

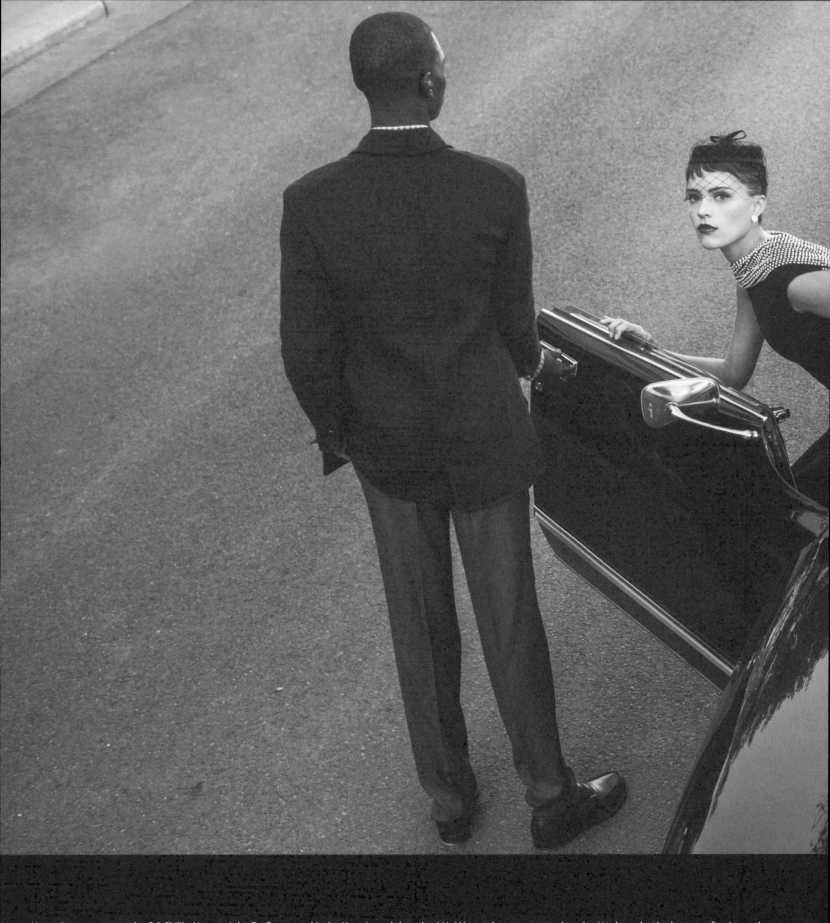

Mamadou wears a coat by 3.1 Phillip Lim, a suit by De Fursac, a shirt by Hermès and shoes by J.M. Weston. Loane wears a dress by Mugler, a hat by Laurence Bossion and earrings by Chanel.

·Fin.

Ryuichi

The celebrated Japanese composer reveals the oddly shaped edges of his constantly questing mind.

Sakamoto

Words by *Charles Shafaieh*, Photography by *Christopher Ferguson* & Styling by *Debbie Hsieh*

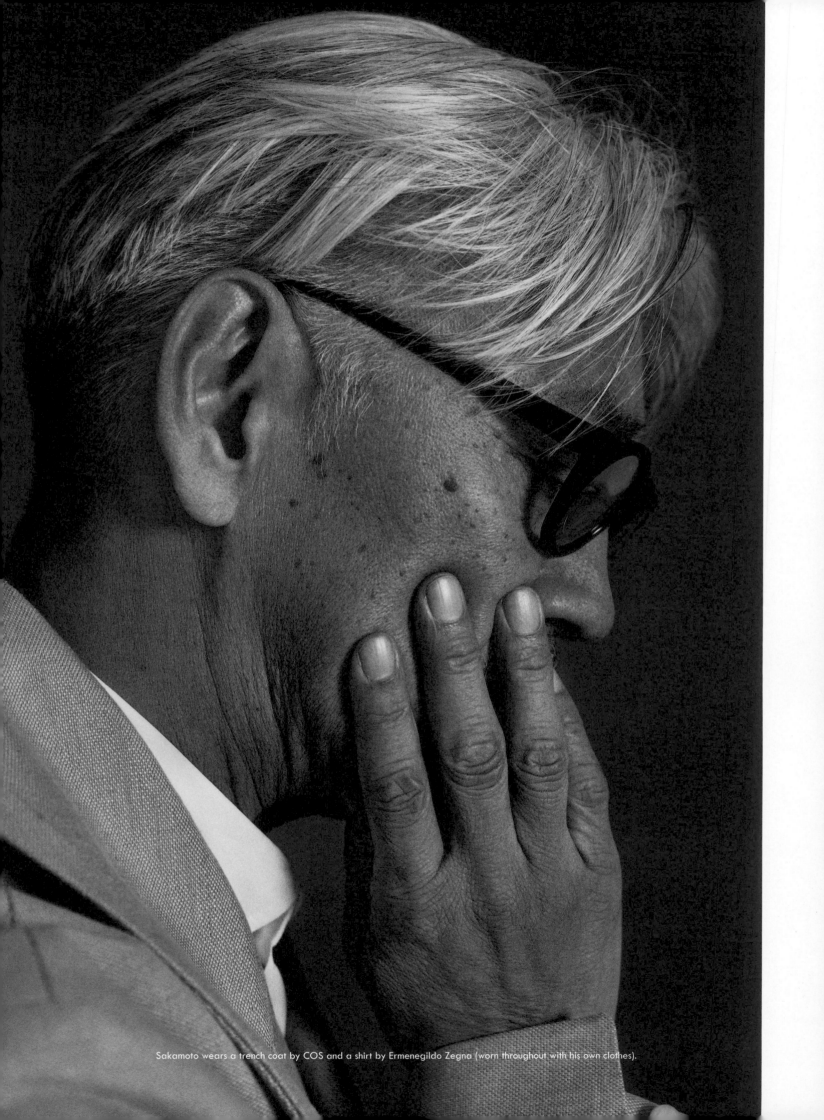

Sakamoto wears a trench coat by COS and a shirt by Ermenegildo Zegna (worn throughout with his own clothes).

Ryuichi Sakamoto is fascinated by the strange sounds made by a piano that survived the 2011 earthquake and tsunami on Japan's eastern seaboard, despite its being thrown about by the water. "I felt as if I was playing the corpse of a piano that had drowned," he says in *Ryuichi Sakamoto: Coda*, a 2017 documentary about his life and work. This fascination is unsurprising, as it serves as an embodiment of many of his passions and predilections, including his endless curiosity for undiscovered sounds, his support for environmental issues and his acute awareness of and sensitivity toward the mortality of all living things—including the planet.

As the first snow of the season fell on lower Manhattan, Sakamoto, the Academy Award–winning composer of such film scores as *The Revenant* and *The Last Emperor* as well as a founding member of the band Yellow Magic Orchestra, sat down to discuss why trauma stops people from listening to music, how he considers his past a series of closed chapters and why he designed a playlist for one of his favorite New York restaurants.

You've said you imagine that Bach, when composing, asked, "Why is there suffering?" Do you ask a question when you write? Bach wrote uplifting music, but his most important works, like *St. Matthew Passion*, sound full of agony to me. I'm sure he was looking at the tragedy and sadness of the people around him. I don't think he was trying to save the world

with his music, but I'm sure it was about prayer. The shock I had after the tsunami and the nuclear plant accident in Japan is still here [he touches his heart]. What was that and what should I do? I still don't have the answer, but I have been trying to help children in those affected areas, bringing them back to music. Most importantly, I'm thinking about those events, and they affect my writing.

Why do you write music at all, considering you seem so fascinated, even consumed, by sounds that exist in nature? It's wasting time to listen to music when you go outside because there are so many interesting noises. For example, every time it rains, I open the window and put the recorder outside. I should always be ready to be surprised, like by the siren of a patrol car in Barcelona and other cities. I hit things, on the street or anywhere, to check the sound—until I find the perfect idea of sound. I haven't found it yet and am always searching.

If I were satisfied listening to nature though, I wouldn't need to write music. I still desire it, so it's contradictory.

Is there too much music today? At university, where I studied ethnomusicology, a professor told me about a concept that I like so much: There used to be many villages in Europe and Asia where there was only one song. That melody, with different lyrics, tells everything from the happiness of a wedding to the

funeral ceremony. It is not made by a person but by time, history and anonymous people. I respect the quality of that music more than music written from money-driven desire in our capitalist world. Of course, there are sincere creators and artists, but I still believe there is too much music.

The right music for the right space seems imperative to you, in your films and also at the restaurant Kajitsu—which you designed a playlist for last year. **What inspired your choices for that project?** The sound should be appropriate to the quality of the food, and also the aesthetic of the space. Maybe the people, too. Kajitsu's food is based on traditional Japanese *kaiseki*—it's very slow and quiet as the dishes are served one by one. It doesn't need bar music and can be nice without music, but maybe some little changes might make the customers feel better. It should be atmospheric—just a

"*Every time it rains, I open the window and put the recorder outside.*"

"Silence's importance is increasing as I'm getting older."

mood. Sometimes I go there just to check the sound levels… and many times I complain that it is too loud!

Such meticulous curation of a soundscape seems connected to your work making ringtones for the phone company Nokia, too. Since the early 1970s, I've been interested in not only music but the soundscape of the city—the noises and signals of our city life. Aside from being asked, that's probably why I made a lot of commercial music for Japanese television in the '70s and '80s. I thought it would be nice to change the Japanese people's sound environment. It's the same reason I worked on the Nokia ringtone: I was so tired of hearing huge sounds from the cellphones in airport lobbies or on the street. That famous ringtone—a huge, loud sound—was ringing everywhere!

Do you have a seminal sound memory? Probably my first memory of film music: When I was four or five years old, I was on my mother's lap in a very dark space—probably a cinema—and I don't remember anything about the film except the theme music and that it was black and white. Each time the radio played that theme, I would jump and say, "That music! That music!" Decades later, I found it was Nino Rota's theme for Fellini's *La Strada*.

Did you think about sounds differently during your years in the Yellow Magic Orchestra than you do today? Listening back to that music, it's so powerful and energetic to me. It was considered very cold—"computer music"—but in fact, 80 percent was manual.

If I were asked to play it today, I couldn't. It was youth. Definitely it's my past—a memory from my life that feels foreign and finished. It's a chapter, and I always want to go forward.

Silence seems more critical for you now. Silence's importance is increasing as I'm getting older. In our busy postmodern cities, we need it for balance, to get our brains empty. People are always getting input, and that means less time for expressing, which is bad. In 2016, when I was making the album *async*, I forbade myself from looking at Facebook and Twitter. Just eating information makes you unable to move.

Extreme silence occurs after tragedies, you've observed—like in New York after September 11. Why would a city react that way? People in New York needed almost one week for the shock to decrease. For about three days, people were searching for their relatives and loved ones, not knowing what to do or what was next. It was very tense. They didn't have the capacity to listen or think about music. Music comes after desperation. That happened to me then, too, and after my cancer diagnosis. [Sakamoto was diagnosed with stage three throat cancer in 2014. He is now in remission.] I was in shock and too tense, maybe. In moments of life and death, there's no possibility to listen to music. It cannot save, unfortunately!

Yet the Irish sing at wakes. Pina Bausch repeatedly said, "Dance! Dance! Otherwise, we are lost." Not only culturally but as people, we need dancing and music, otherwise we are lost.

A VERY LONG ENGAGEMENT

TEXT:
ELLIE VIOLET BRAMLEY

Marriage is a shape-shifting institution. Before people dreamt of white weddings, they dreamt of social advancement, strategic alliances and, if they were lucky, some pleasant company along the way. Then Cupid aimed his arrow at the heart of the establishment, and romance and marriage became as intertwined as the proverbial horse and carriage. Taking the long view, Ellie Violet Bramley *asks: What's love got to do with it?*

"I love a great love story," Meghan Markle told an interviewer a few weeks before she and Prince Harry announced their engagement. Their wedding, months later, was watched by a global audience that ran into the hundreds of millions. "Two people fell in love and we all showed up," read one headline. A more sweeping advertisement for the partnership between love and marriage would be hard to come by: This was the fairy tale of romantic attraction transforming, via white wedding, into marital bliss.

But love has not always been the bedrock for entering into marriage that it is across swathes of the world today. Throughout history, it has played different roles: from a happy by-product to a threat to social order. In the Hindu tradition, notes historian Stephanie Coontz, author of *Marriage, a History: How Love Conquered Marriage*, love is celebrated in marriage, but has not always been considered a legitimate reason for marriage. Muslim and Christian thinkers alike have, at times, thought of love and intimacy in marriage as a threat to godly devotion.

Marriage is a millennia-old institution, but it is not an immovable one. It has, in fact, shape-shifted over time—despite the collective cultural amnesia that tells us it was always thus.

"Even a cursory scan through the historical and anthropological record reveals that the nuclear family that most Americans think of as normal—one spawned when reciprocal romantic love inspires one man and one woman to exchange vows to forsake all others... is quite the cultural exception rather than the rule," writes Judith Stacey, a professor of social and cultural analysis at New York University, in her 2011 book *Unhitched*.

Is romantic love an entirely modern phenomenon? It has, of course, always existed in some form or another. Coontz argues that "every society that we know of has recognized the existence of romantic love." It's just that most societies, she writes, "have been very suspicious of that as a motive for marriage."

Some scholars, such as John Witte, a professor of law and ethics at Emory University, are keen to push back on a reading that paints love in marriage as a modern phenomenon. Over the phone from Georgia, the author of *From Sacrament to Contract: Marriage, Religion, and Law in the Western Tradition* says that while romantic love was not a sine qua non, in the "average interaction between a man and a woman who decide to get married, love is part of the calculus." And yet, it seems that by and large, it was not sufficient to trump other factors in the way it does today.

Meanwhile, who could marry whom has always been regulated. Canadian historian Elizabeth Abbott points out that in every community there are restrictions that "stem from each society's view of itself and its people... Aristocrats married aristocrats and peasants married peasants; Christians married Christians and Jews married Jews," and so on. Tough luck if you fell in love with someone deemed unacceptable, or, of course, bar in a few cultures, if you didn't fit into the restrictive heterosexual mold.

Literature testifies to the long and lustrous history of romantic love—a quick scan from Shakespeare to Rumi will serve up ample examples of young lovers, star-crossed lovers, illicit lovers. But romantic love, explains Stacey over Skype, was "usually outside of marriage."

The trope of the lovers restricted by familial responsibility and forced to marry for money or social status rather than love are abundant: from Romeo and Juliet to the novels of Jane Austen.

If romantic love was not the primary reason for marriage, what was? "When you look at all the things that marriage does and doesn't do across cultures, the one thing that it has in common," says Coontz, "is that it creates in-laws." That, so her argument goes, is the main reason that marriage was invented. Families and communities, bound—for better or worse—through marital ties, would want to hold huge sway over who was allowed to marry whom. Coontz's book elucidates the various ways in which family—as well as closely entwined economic and political—considerations have dominated marriage throughout history. To name a few: It has been used to "create new ties of kinship," "to build far-flung personal networks that gave people access to hunting, natural resources or water holes in other regions," and to turn "strangers into relatives and enemies into allies."

All across the ancient world, from the Middle East to Africa, India to China, Central to South America, and over the course of thousands of years, marriage for aristocrats and emperors—made distinct by cultural practices—was seen as a key mechanism for what we might now call political hustling. A similar thing was happening among the less fancy folk of the ancient world who put economics ahead of personal satisfaction. The notion of what you needed in and from a marriage was, throughout history, explains Stacey, "much more related to production, reproduction, family economy, the right sort of people, family stability, intergenerational stability—many, many things." So far, so unromantic. Many of the most seismic shifts when it comes to the shape of marriage had little to do with romantic love. Religions have caused big rumblings, each supporting different models of marriage. Early Christianity, for example, had initial suspicions that marriage, in the words of Coontz, "undermined the rigorous self-control needed to achieve spiritual salvation." But with the fall of the Roman empire, the church became increasingly involved in marriage politics, which were crucial to the struggle for power.

So how did the shift to the idea of marrying for love and not, at best, with love as a fortunate consequence, take root? It's hard to pin down. Indeed, in many societies it is still not the norm. The love match has the hardest time establishing "in areas where you still have very high levels of extended family systems that are a central part of the economic and political organization," says Coontz. "Japan made the transition during the '50s and '60s from arranged marriages, India is moving toward that—still many marriages are arranged but kids have much more veto power than they used to."

Coontz identifies the Victorians as "the first people in history to try to make marriage the pivotal experience in people's lives," but with women still largely dependent on their husbands' wages, "many saw marriage as the only alternative to destitution or prostitution." It was hardly a recipe for love conquering all. So romantic ideals continued to be stymied by gender roles and the practical considerations that went with them.

For Stacey, romantic love as the priority in marriage is a 20th-century phenomenon. The shifts in gender relations and the centrality of sexuality in the first two decades helped change the terms of relationships. Marriage on more equal terms was actually becoming a possibility. "It happens much more in cities," says Stacey. "One of the important aspects of urbanization is sexual migration." You may, in the past, have gotten lucky and fallen for someone in your town or existing social circle, but cities stack the numbers in your favor; plus away from the grip of older generations you have the freedom to act. Of course, marriage was still restricted for many members of society—in the US, for example, a considerable number of states still had statutes that prohibited interracial marriage.

The 1950s were, in some ways, a golden era for the nuclear family setup. "In this unique period in western history," writes Coontz, "marriage provided the context for just about every piece of most people's lives." Yet it remained largely based on the mold of previous eras: "The cultural consensus that everyone should marry and form a male breadwinner family was like a steamroller that crushed every alternative view." So women were still making decisions based at least in part on status and livelihood.

Marriage based on the more egalitarian—and individualistic—take on romantic love that we now might expect, or at least hope for in an ideal world, is in part a product of the shifts that took place throughout the '60s and '70s. And that was the point at which, Coontz argues, marriage lost its role as the "master

event." She explains, "People began marrying later and premarital sex became the norm." Things were shifting away from the male breadwinner model that had taken more than 150 years to become "the dominant model in North America and Western Europe" and which took "less than 25 years to dismantle." Even though marriage may no longer be the only peak of people's lives—it now jostles for space next to careers, friendships and sexual freedoms—all of these metamorphoses have worked to solidify the place of love within marriage.

And with many countries extending the right to marry to same-sex couples in the last few decades, marriage has finally allowed for a more inclusive view of romantic love. In the introduction to Unhitched, Stacey notes, "Love, marriage, and baby carriages are all the rage among lesbians, gay men, and transgender people." She says that since they were excluded from the institution for so long, "The drive for same-sex marriage became the centerfold campaign of a vigorous gay rights movement."

The male breadwinner model may endure in many heterosexual households to this day. But according to Coontz, by the end of the last century, a majority of women told pollsters that love—not money or status or power—trumped all other considerations when it came to marrying. So even if marriage has lost some of its former potency, love within marriage is more valued than ever. Of course for many people, economic factors never entirely disappear.

"One of the paradoxes and sad ironies of the relationship between feminism and the mass employment of women," says Stacey, "is that we now have much greater class inequality."

"Where marriages used to come with familial and community relationships built in for support, partnerships based wholly on romantic love have morphed marriage into a unit of two—placing a lot of weight on two sets of shoulders."

Marriage, she argues, used to be an indirect redistribution system, but now "likes marry likes and two high-earners marry and two low-earners marry." In the US context at least, with the gap between rich and poor so vast and "a lot of people at the lower end unable to self-support, it's hard to make romantic love the main factor."

For those for whom a more egalitarian love-match marriage is an option, the new model of this millennia-old institution can be difficult to uphold. Once perceived as the entry into adult life, now it is one option of many as people customize their life choices—from living alone to cohabiting and having children out of wedlock—rather than bending to the one-size-fits-all model of the past. Coontz says this is being felt in almost all industrialized countries.

Compared to previous rationales for marriage, "individual romantic love is clearly the least stable," according to Stacey. It has, she says, an internal contradiction: "We base marriage in contemporary so-called western societies enormously on the notion of the chemistry between two people, a certain kind of erotic compatibility or romantic attraction and that's a pretty weak read for knowing if you're compatible in ways that last."

With scholars describing a rise in "expressive individualism" since the late '60s, the idea that our societal obligations play second fiddle to our personal desires means that if we fall out of love, the pressure to stay in a loveless—or even just love-lite—marriage is less. Some have described this as the era of the self-expressive marriage. As psychology professor Eli Finkel puts it, at least in an American context, people "now look to marriage increasingly for self-dis-covery, self-esteem and personal growth." It's a tall order for a marriage still to be providing ripe terrain for self-discovery 40 years in.

Expectations of marriage have in many cases been dramatically elevated. Look to the wedding industry for evidence; it's a lens onto the way a culture views marriage. With the average wedding in the US now costing upwards of $25,000, for instance, the fireworks of The Big Day itself correspond to the hyperbolized romantic ideals we have come to pin on it.

These heightened expectations have led to what Finkel has called "the all-or-nothing marriage." He notes, "The average marriage today is weaker than the average marriage of yore, in terms of both satisfaction and divorce rate, but the best marriages today are much stronger, in terms of both satisfaction and personal well-being." So contemporary marriage is a difficult institution to uphold precisely because so much is expected of it. Marriage now comes with a mandate for happiness that if not met, could be used to justify its own end.

In this age of romantic love, we are also piling a lot onto our marital sex lives in ways we likely wouldn't have in the past. In The State of Affairs, psychotherapist Esther Perel writes: "Today we are engaged in a grand experiment. For the first time ever, we want sex with our spouses not just because we want six children to work on the farm... nor because it is an assigned chore." Marital intimacy now, she argues, has become nothing short of "the sovereign antidote for lives of growing atomization." No pressure then.

Where marriages used to come with familial and community relationships built in for sup-port, partnerships based wholly on romantic love have morphed marriage into a unit of two—placing a lot of weight on two sets of shoulders.

Our feelings of significance as individuals, Perel asserts, hinge on the ability of our partners to share intimacy with us and only us in ways that wouldn't have been expected—particularly of men—in marriages of the past. She notes, marital monogamy was "a mainstay of patriarchy, imposed on women to ensure patrimony and lineage."

Modern ideas of monogamy might conversely make modern marriage harder to maintain. Where it used to mean one person for life, "Now monogamy means one person at a time," Perel writes. On average, people marry later in life, having sown their wild oats, so to speak. The logic goes that this will make monogamous marriages easier to uphold. But, in today's culture in which individual fulfillment comes fully mandated, Perel notes, "never have we been more tempted to stray."

Love and marriage now exist in a unique social context. For one, the very modern feeling of FOMO (fear of missing out) is not limited to missed house parties. While the internet might be a notoriously rocky place to date, it certainly adds an awareness of ever-present options being but a swipe (and an Uber) away.

Marriage has, by and large, become less practical and more loving, more of a choice and therefore less resilient. We have become more romantic and egalitarian about marital love while being simultaneously more pragmatic. Romantic love as the basis for marriage is a vote for optimism and hope precisely because it is such a volatile—and optional—one.

Day in the Life:
Mona Kowalska

How do you build a brand that can weather fashion's changing seasons and fickle loyalties?
Tahirah Hairston speaks to the founder of A Détacher about the long-term benefits of dodging hype, staying small and working four-day weeks. Photography by *Zoltan Tombor*

FEATURES

Mona Kowalska's studio sits right below her shop on Mulberry Street, an area within walking distance of some of the coolest independent brands in New York City—Noah, Creatures of Comfort, No.6—and far enough away from the hustle and bustle of the chain-store fashion purgatory of SoHo for her to catch a glimpse of tranquility. When I meet her, the designer is in the middle of creating patterns for A Détacher's next collection (she makes all of her own prints too), figuring out the right draping for a shirt she plans to include. "This was many, many muslins," she says, showing me the most recent iteration.

Hanging on racks alongside the walls of her studio are the patterns from her past 20 collections—massive pieces of eggshell-white paper with intricate blue or black markings. It goes like this: First, she drapes a dress form with muslin and marks up the fabric with darts and seams, then she traces around the fabric on a large piece of paper to create the pattern. It's a process that is repeated many, many times until Kowalska gets the right fit. "I make things that I can't necessarily draw, so it's not something I can delegate," she explains. The arduous draping means Kowalska usually grades everything too—meaning, in layman's terms, she does all the sizing.

It's a rarity for a fashion designer with 20 years in the game to be so hands-on, but essential to the DNA of Kowalska as a businesswoman. "I know there's this idea that I'm an intentionally small brand," Kowalska says. "But I've just made certain choices about how I want to work, which I suppose dictated a lot of other decisions." The result is having a staff of only three, and a four-day workweek. "I think you need one day for cultural pursuits, one day of idleness and then another day to just take care of your life," she says. That her collection is limited as a result of her working practices feels like a positive: "For me there is the best expression of an idea, not five expressions of the same idea to see which one hits," she says.

Kowalska has been able to not only maintain A Détacher as a sustainable brand, but a cool one. Rather than "hype"—a marketing tactic brands use to keep consumers engaged by building momentum around limited-release and on-the-nose collaborations—"cool" is less easy to define. For Kowalska, it translates to being understated and drawing attention through authenticity. "It's like when somebody sings a song that is just perfectly suited for their voice, and they clearly know their range

Kowalska sometimes draws on literary inspiration for her designs. The smock dresses and chunky knits of her 2015 fall collection were a tribute to Elena Ferrante's Neapolitan Novels.

"For me there is the best expression of an idea, not five expressions."

and the phrasing. Sometimes, you see someone dressed like that," she explains. She has, perhaps unintentionally, mastered it herself by staying true to her modus operandi. In a cream alpaca cardigan, a black ribbed jumpsuit tied at the waist as pants, clogs and a blue floral scarf around her neck, the platinum-blonde designer is a poster woman for her brand.

She's built A Détacher, which means "to be detached" in French, on the idea that women should feel good in their clothing. Bold prints, cozy knits, architectural silhouettes, and quirky details that make her designs feel special have attracted a loyal fan base of women who want to please themselves, and—like Kowalska and the cream cardigan she's been wearing for the past several weeks—repeat their outfits. "When something feels good, I'll wear it for weeks on end like a maniac," she says. "I just think, 'That worked yesterday, and it'll work today.'"

Growing up in communist Poland until age nine, where her mother worked as the head of an atelier at one of the big clothing factories and also saw private clients at home, Kowalska got her first insights into what women wore and what it meant to subtly stand out. "It was a very feminine environment. Women coming in for fittings and leaving their perfume behind in the house," she says. There wasn't much variation in clothing ("The small would be black, the medium would be red and the large would be yellow, and you'd have to pick from that"). Items that weren't readily available were more desirable—like the red clogs Kowalska's mother found on the black market, or the gray dress she joined Girl Scouts in order to possess or the jeans that her mother made from scratch.

All of these items were memorable because they stood out from the mundane, which encapsulates Kowalska's approach to A Détacher. She doesn't want to make clothes for everybody or clothes that can be easily forgotten. "I just want to make your favorite thing because that's what I want for myself," she says.

After moving to Baltimore for high school (where she became an expert in thrift shopping) and studying political science at the University of Chicago, Kowalska moved to Italy to study fashion at a technical school in Florence. She didn't go with a particular plan in mind, but after graduation she worked in Italy and Paris for a few small brands including Sonia Rykiel, beefing up her knitwear and tailoring skills. In 1998, after doing a few of her own collections with a partner in Italy, she relaunched A Détacher in New York City as a bricks-and-mortar store. Ten years later, she had her first official New York Fashion Week show. "For me, it was my livelihood and it had to have longevity. I was

really putting everything into it—I used all my savings. My daughter was two when I opened this business. It couldn't not work," says Kowalska.

It's been working for 20 years, and Kowalska gets inspiration from everything surrounding her—politics (there's a Hillary Clinton poster still up on the wall in the store), her personal life, philosophy, famous criminal cases (there was a collection inspired by Patty Hearst), literature (right now, she's reading Fleur Jaeggy) and naps. Even after two decades, comfort still trumps ambitious design imperatives: "When you like something and you feel good in it, you should be able to take a nap in it and then get up and be fine," she says.

Sharon

Van

Photography by *Katie McCurdy* & Styling by *Ashley Abtahie*

Harriet Fitch Little speaks to *Sharon Van Etten* about new music, motherhood and going back to school.

Etten

Sharon Van Etten must surely be the most popular student at Brooklyn College. In the past decade the singer —turned mature sophomore—has released five albums, toured the world with them, and made fans cry with the melancholy of her music.

FEATURES

In fact, a large part of the reason Van Etten is back in school is for the sake of her adoring masses: The music she writes prompts such confessional fervor among audiences that, she says, she felt she owed it to them to get some professional training in mental health counseling.

But the lecture hall packs a tougher crowd than any music auditorium. "I think I'm seen as the old person in class and they're like, 'Why [is she] here?... I don't want to sit next to her because she might take herself too seriously or something,'" says Van Etten who, at 38, is only old by the standards of someone still suffering from teenage acne.

Like most people who could be described, non-ironically, as "cool," Van Etten doesn't much mind that this particular crowd doesn't recognize her as such. She has bigger fish to fry. First, the new music: Her album *Remind Me Tomorrow* was released in January, and she'll be skipping class this spring to tour it in the US and Europe. She's also been dabbling in acting: first with a role in the Netflix supernatural series *The OA* (playing—no surprise—a woman gifted with a magical voice) and then in season three of David Lynch's *Twin Peaks* in which she performed on stage at the fictional Roundhouse Inn—the holy grail of hipster cameos. She's also taken a shine to stand-up comedy (more on that later) and wants to try scriptwriting with a babysitter she got to know in Los Angeles. And where there's talk of a babysitter there is, of course, a baby: Van Etten has a toddler, who she is raising with her drummer-turned-manager boyfriend in Brooklyn's leafy Carroll Gardens neighborhood.

In sum: Life is busy, happy—and increasingly domestic. This might be strange for Van Etten, who named her 2012 breakthrough album *Tramp* in honor of the amount of time she spent crashing on friends' sofas while writing it. "[Previously], every time the tour cycle came around, I would give up my apartment and when my touring was done I would move again," she recalls, speaking over Skype from her living room. Her apartment is technically a two-bedroom but really "a one-bedroom with a walk-in closet" (the baby sleeps in the closet), and yet she describes it as "the most adult apartment I've ever had."

Van Etten has built a career on writing songs about life's most turbulent moments, with lyrics that dice the raw horror of heartbreak with the precision of a sushi chef wielding a freshly sharpened knife. "Break my legs so I won't walk to you/ Cut my tongue so I can't talk to you/ Burn my skin so I can't feel you/ Stab my eyes so I can't see," she sings on "Your Love is Killing Me" (2014). But she has always been a clear-eyed advocate for a mature sort of sadness: a melancholy that doesn't beg to be immediately resolved but folded into the mix of life. "I want it to be cool to be sad," she said in an interview in 2009, shortly after moving to New York. "People don't allow themselves to be sad, and I think it's all right."

Van Etten didn't release her first album until she was 28—a relatively slow start that perhaps contributed to the maturity of her lyrics. What happened before that first release? "I kind of went my own way for a while," she says. After finishing high school in New Jersey in 1999, she left home as quickly as possible. "I was just an angsty kid for no reason and I wanted to get the fuck out as soon as I could," she says. (In retrospect, she describes the large family she left behind—she is the middle

"I'm fine with the narrative, but I'm not that sad person anymore."

child of five—as "very healthy.") But rather than heading straight for the bright lights of New York City, Van Etten ended up in Murfreesboro, Tennessee, a town whose only dent in popular culture is as the setting for the 2014 film *Tammy*—in which Melissa McCarthy's character is bent on leaving it. Van Etten enrolled in the local university to study recording but dropped out. She had a job in a music café and a boyfriend in a local emo band ("No one anyone would know, except in that very small town," is how she politely dismisses it). She only sang at open mic night when he was away, because he disliked her performing her "too personal" songs in public. The relationship wasn't just creatively stifling; it was also abusive.

Six years after leaving New Jersey, Van Etten found herself back on her family's doorstep. The prodigal daughter's return was met with cautious enthusiasm. "Everyone was happy I was back and wanted to do everything they could to help me, but, I think in the back of their minds they were preparing themselves for me to leave again—because I wasn't in a good mental space," Van Etten explains. So, her room and board came with three stipulations: that she get therapy, find a job and re-enroll in school.

The stage seemed set for a life of suburban stability, but Van Etten got lucky. It turned out that her therapist was a former jazz singer, and completely sold on the idea that her new patient should move to New York to pursue music "because she could tell how much it was helping me." The job she found in New Jersey—in a liquor store—helped her get a good position in a wine shop when she did take the leap and move to the city. And, during her brief stint back at college studying photography, she took the photo that would become the cover of her album *Are We There*—a black and white picture of her friend leaning out the window of a moving car. "Everything ties in," she concludes, with obvious satisfaction.

Van Etten worked for a while in music PR, so she has a keen sense of how a powerful backstory can be used to pigeonhole an artist's output—sometimes helpfully, sometimes not. What does she think of how the media spins her story?

"I'm fine with the narrative as long as the preface is that I'm not that sad person anymore and that I've come a long way," she says.

The question, then, is: What does a singer best known for being sad do when they're happy? This is what Van Etten grapples with on *Remind Me Tomorrow*, right from the first line of the new album's first song. In "I Told You Everything" she sings: "Sitting at a bar, I told you everything/ You said 'Holy shit, You almost died.'" This was a real exchange—the first intimate conversation that Van Etten had with the man who is now her partner, and father of her son. "I told him a story that maybe I'll tell one day in the public eye, but I don't know when I'll be ready," she explains.

["It's] a big part of my life from my early 20s and one of the main reasons I went home." But the lyrics are also a declaration to her fans that she has moved on. As she puts it: "This is me talking to you. This is me trying to tell you that this is how it started, but I'm okay now."

The reaction of her own publicist on hearing the new album: "Holy shit!" (but in a good way, Van Etten is quick to add). Sonically, it feels huge—strident, orchestral, instrumentally and electronically layered. She says the change in sound is down to producer John Congleton, who has previously worked with acts including St. Vincent and The Walkmen. "If I had tried to make it myself, I would have made a record like *Are We There*," she says. (Her last album, which reached number 25 on the Billboard charts, was produced by Van Etten herself.) "I sang everything and I played here and there [on *Remind Me Tomorrow*] but I didn't play guitar, which is really wild," she adds. It's a bold move for a singer best known for her acoustic performances: "I don't think that it's so far from myself that it's going to be shocking to people, or that I'll alienate my fans [although] I have this small personal fear every time I make a record."

Those same fans would be doubly shocked to know that Van Etten is moonlighting as an amateur comedian; last year she performed a stand-up set in Los Angeles and wants to get into writing skits. Her comedy material, like her life in Carroll Gardens, is light and domestic in tone—"kind of mom-centric," is how she puts it apologetically. There's a joke about trying to make friends with other parents in the park, and another about what her toddler's Tinder profile might look like. "It's still a work in progress, but I have all these small ideas and we'll see where it ends up," she says. At least the set in Los Angeles went well. "People laughed," she says—although she adds that it was "probably because of how nervous and awkward I was."

Talking to Van Etten, an impression builds of someone who would have to try—really try—to alienate her fans. People seem to just like her; from comedy audiences (not famed for their tolerance toward newbies), to the directors who sought her out for roles despite her total lack of acting experience, to the scores of musicians who have helped her along the way—The National, Beirut and Bon Iver among them.

Is Van Etten aware that she's someone who attracts people to her? "I think because I'm introverted by nature people can talk to me because I'm a good listener," she says, adding, "Middle child status helped me learn how to be a mediator."

It's easy to imagine Van Etten as a therapist when she parses her personal history like this, and once she gets her degree in mental health counseling she will be exactly that. But, like everything else, she'll take her own sweet time about getting there. "I'm giving myself until I'm 50," she says. "It's going to take a long time if I'm doing everything else I want to be doing."

At Work With:
Kyle Abraham

In a New York studio, the choreographer dances, rehearses and breaks down the meaning of his "postmodern gumbo" technique with *Djassi DaCosta Johnson*. Photography by *Zoltan Tombor*

"I would love to be in a place to make a dance about flowers and just be 'pretty.'"

In a rehearsal studio at New York Live Arts, Kyle Abraham is leading his dancers like a conductor. He moves his fingers in sync with their legs as they dance through the space in athletic, sinuous formations. At one point he begins dancing himself; gliding into the middle of the room, his body alternating between animated pop-like sequences and languid balletic undulations. "Yes!" he says. The room buzzes as the dancers finish the piece, clapping for each other and collapsing to the floor. Abraham pauses, then asks with a smile, "Are you okay?"

Abraham, born in Pittsburgh, Pennsylvania, knows the two sides of this relationship equally well. In his 20s, he worked as a dancer for various companies before striking out in 2006 and founding his own: Abraham In Motion. In the 13 years since, he has built a fan base—and been the recipient of awards including a MacArthur Fellowship—for his choreography, which incorporates a powerful understanding of American vernacular movement. He has used his platform to comment on the human condition and the black experience in America, while also challenging sexual stereotypes.

We sat down before his rehearsal to talk about his most recent, celebrated, work for New York City Ballet—"A paragon of outsider infiltration," in the words of one *Financial Times* critic—and what it will take to break the patriarchy within the dance world.

You're a choreographer, but also a dancer in your own right. Do you have a daily dance practice? I call what I do a "postmodern gumbo" because I'm taking things from all different modern dance techniques and genres, and kind of using them as a movement vocabulary. My warmup varies and depends on if I'm dancing. If I'm going to be dancing or doing some of my own work that day, I'll probably do my own warmup that I've made up. If it's a rehearsal, I like to start with my goals for the day, just writing them down for a little bit of clarity, and then I'll dive into the physical practice.

What inspires your choreography? I play with gesture in different ways, and with found movement—movement that's in everyday cultures. Hopefully, when people who are from those backgrounds come to the ballet and see the movement, [they'll] be like, "Oh, you know, I saw myself for the first time in the ballet."

Choreographers who have come before you, such as Bill T. Jones and Ralph Lemon, have dealt with their work being politicized. How do you feel about that? I'm not living with such an abundance of privilege that I can't see the injustices that are happening in this world. I would love to be in a place to make a dance about flowers and just be "pretty"—I think that's also needed—but, for me, I'm trying to work out a lot of things in the work that I make. Luckily, I'm coming from a time where I was able to see artists like Bill T. Jones or Bebe Miller or Ralph Lemon or Ishmael Houston-Jones—this legacy of black dance-makers. I am aware of the responsibility and I'm also aware of how what I'm doing and saying can be read.

Your work is known for being about an awareness of the "self" in society. What work do you feel compelled to make at this moment of incredible strife in our country? I'm in the middle of a four-part process. The first work is really focused on black love. It's premiering in 2020 and uses the music of D'Angelo. The next work, probably in 2022, is talking about black community, and that's using Kendrick Lamar. The next is 2026, when we're thinking about black folks' relationship with faith and religion, and it's all gospel music. From there, inspired by Ohad [Naharin]'s work, I'm taking the "B-side" sections that won't make it to the actual evening-length piece of [those three works] and making them part of a fourth project.

On working with New York City Ballet, Abraham says, "I felt pressure to represent so many different worlds."

Congratulations on your premiere of *The Runaway* with New York City Ballet. It's huge news for the dance community on many levels. Can you speak to your experience setting a work for a classical ballet company? I was definitely challenged by pointe work. I did feel like I had to choreograph *en pointe* because there was expectation, and there are also people that want to dismiss me, right? So, I had to attack it and just say, "Okay, I'm going to make some pointe work!" It may not be revolutionary, but I don't have to make a revolutionary dance. I just have to make a dance that goes over well and that represents me.

I noticed you used both contemporary and classical music in *The Runaway*. Was your own classical music background in cello and piano comforting and helpful when working with City Ballet? With the classical music, it was really funny. I mean, of course I can read music, but a lot of people didn't know much about my background and didn't actually know that. Although I often work with contemporary popular music, it doesn't mean that I don't know classical music or know how to work with measure, and all these different things.

You recently refused work on an all-male bill. That personal activism can be very powerful. It's kind of scary to think that these directors, a lot of times, are not going outside. They're just hearing a whisper from a friend in the elite boys' clubs, or waiting for a review of something—which is a really particular perspective on what's good and what's valid in the world. I think it's really, really important for directors and curators to realize that there is a major difference between highlighting and segregating. And that's what happens all too often. Having an all-women choreographer tribute one night is not integrating them into the program every night.

Collaboration seems particularly important to your work. I feel like a choreographer's job is the same as a host at a dinner party. You want to make sure everyone's having a good time. If you're so distracted by looking at negative energy or ego, it's taking away from the work. In working with my dancers as collaborators, I may be setting the steps—but I am in

"A choreographer's job is the same as a host at a dinner party."

conversation. I'll have them write down their favorite section in a secret ballot. It gives me perspective to think about how they're viewing the importance of certain moments in that work. Their input influences what the work becomes.

You are one of the few dance companies that employs your dancers full time and provides health insurance. That can't be easy, or everyone would do it. Why did you feel that was important? I don't know if there's an eloquent answer. I can't even give the dancers what they deserve. They should be paid much more than they're paid and health insurance is something everyone should have. What's being asked of them is monumental. How do you not give them health insurance?

What kind of legacy would you like for your work? I want to make work that can stand up 10 years, 20 years, 50 years and 100 years from now. I don't really know if I've done that—I hope I have. I want people to be able to say, "Wow, in 2012 this black choreographer made a piece called *Pavement*. This is what was happening in America. And now in 2112, look where we are." It's important for us to be able to look back, you know?

Abraham has a rule of turning down offers to work on mixed bills that don't feature a woman choreographer. "Who's on the ground looking for new voices?" he asks.

Archive:
Langston Hughes

Left Photograph: © H. Cartier Bresson/Magnum Photos/Scanpix Denmark, Right Photograph: Unknown/Scanpix Denmark

"I, too, sing America," *Langston Hughes* wrote in 1926. He sang the country to many tunes: as an author, playwright, journalist and—above all—as the preeminent poet of the Harlem Renaissance. *Neda Semnani* charts the life of the merchant sailor turned Literary colossus.

"Above all, Hughes was a poet. He wrote on and on, until he ran clear out of days."

In a train outside of St. Louis sat a young Langston Hughes. He had graduated from high school some weeks earlier and, though he should have been excited for the big life about to unfold before him, he was in a melancholic and reflective mood. He stared out of the window, considering the great Mississippi River moving southward into the heart of segregated America.

He thought of his father, a black man whom Hughes believed hated both his blackness and his people. As Hughes looked over the river, he remembered the story he had once read about President Lincoln floating on a raft down the Mississippi and then he thought of other powerful waterways that feature prominently in the history of black Americans.

He pulled out an envelope from his pocket, turned it over and began to write a poem. It begins: "I've known rivers:/ I've known rivers ancient as the world and older than the flow of human blood in human veins./ My soul has grown deep like the rivers." The full poem, "The Negro Speaks of Rivers," set the course for Hughes' exuberant and expansive life, as poet and wanderer.

"He's the poet of dreams," explains Renée Watson, a writer, educator, performer and the founder of the I, Too Arts Collective, a Harlem nonprofit guided by Hughes' principles and housed in his old brownstone. "He's always looking forward and dreaming of what America can be, of what this world can be but not at the cost of being in denial of how things are," she says. "There is a complicated world that he's addressing in his poems."

James Langston Hughes was born in 1902, in Joplin, Missouri, the only son of two difficult and restless souls. His father, John Nathaniel Hughes, left the family when Langston was barely walking, choosing a self-imposed exile in Toluca, Mexico instead. He believed racism in the United States was endemic to its culture and

national character; there was no way for a black person to achieve true upward mobility or financial stability in the States. So, he left and didn't come back.

Langston's mother, Carrie Mercer Langston Hughes, a sometime poet and amateur actress from an illustrious African-American family, was often absent, forced to travel to find work. Langston spent most of his early life in Lawrence, Kansas, with his maternal grandmother, Mary Langston. "[She] held me on her lap," he recalled in his memoir, *The Big Sea*, "and told me long beautiful stories about people who wanted to make the Negroes free." Mary's first husband was killed in an abolitionist's raid on Harpers Ferry, Virginia. Her second was a prestigious abolitionist and brother to John Mercer Langston, one of the first African-Americans elected to Congress after the Civil War.

"I was unhappy for a long time, and very lonesome, living with my grandmother," Hughes writes. "It was then that books began to happen to me, and I began to believe in nothing but books and the wonderful world of books—where if people suffered, they suffered in beautiful language, not in monosyllables, as we did in Kansas."

These early years awoke in Hughes a fiercely private and independent streak. He became a poet at 13 when his classmates unanimously elected him to the office of class poet, because they figured one of the two black kids in class must have rhythm. By high school, he had started publishing verse in the school magazine. After graduation, and against the wishes of his mother, he was desperate to enroll in college. His mother thought it better he get a job to support her. His father wanted him to move to Switzerland where he could study mining engineering; he picked up three more languages—French, German and Italian—along the way.

But Hughes, that once-lonesome boy, had begun to dream of New

While working as a busboy at a hotel in Washington D.C., Hughes slipped some of his poems to the influential poet Vachel Lindsay. His ongoing support helped propel Hughes to mainstream success.

York. "I had an overwhelming desire to see Harlem. More than Paris, or the Shakespeare country, or Berlin, or the Alps, I wanted to see Harlem, the greatest Negro city in the world."

When he got there, as a young man barely 20, he felt like he had come home. Downtown, the Jazz Age was in full swing. Uptown, Harlem was the pulsating epicenter of African-American music, arts and culture. It was the Harlem Renaissance and it was a movement, one that wasn't confined to northern Manhattan but reached cities like Philadelphia, Washington and Paris. For Hughes, who had spent most of his life in mostly white or mixed-race spaces, experiencing a vibrant and reverberating majority black metropolitan neighborhood was a revelation.

"Harlem was a sacred place," explained Watson. "It was this mecca for black people, for our voices to be heard, for us to push back against the status quo and to put our own stories on the record. There was something really powerful about these artists of all art forms taking the mic back, and deciding for themselves, 'This is who we are. This is where we're from. This is how we feel. Stop speaking for us or on behalf of us.'"

Here in Harlem, among a community of young artists and thinkers, Hughes was able to perfect his skills of observation and his ability to sketch the people he saw there in verse and through rhythm. He had always loved his African-American heritage, but there is a sense that, during this period, he fell in love with Blackness—personally and expansively.

In 1926, he wrote his manifesto: "The Negro Artist and the Racial Mountain." It is a brief but soaring call to arms and declaration of intent. The Harlem Renaissance had matured. It was about to send young black men and women, artists and intellectuals all, into the wide world where they would come into their own, as they developed and projected their voices and stories.

He wrote: "We younger Negro artists who create now intend to express our individual darkskinned selves without fear or shame. If white people are pleased we are glad. If they are not, it doesn't matter. We know we are beautiful. And ugly too." He continued, "If colored people are pleased we are glad. If they are not, their displeasure doesn't matter either. We build our temples for tomorrow, strong as we know how, and we stand on top of the mountain, free within ourselves."

Over the course of five decades, Hughes was a Parisian busboy and a gallivanting sailor on a merchant ship. He was an oysterman in a Washington restaurant, and a farmhand on Staten Island. He sailed to Africa, traveled to the farthest East, and crisscrossed Russia.

He was a two-time memoirist, a novelist, and writer of short stories. He was a children's book author, a playwright and a librettist. Hughes filed stories from ships and deep in war zones. He wrote scripts for radio, film and television. He testified before the House Un-American Activities Committee, and lived to write the tale.

He was a prolific translator of Spanish, French, Russian, and even Chinese poetry. He curated anthology after anthology, and introduced the world to the voices of Gwendolyn Brooks and Alice Walker. And he wrote reams of correspondence to friends, acquaintances, colleagues, critics and fans. But above all this he was a poet. Hughes wrote on and on, until he ran clear out of days.

"When I think of Langston Hughes, I think of making a way out of no way," Watson says. "[His attitude was]: 'Hustle. I'm going to figure out a way to get my stories told.' He was the poet who persisted, no matter what."

"My poetry," Hughes said, "on the whole, is very simple." It is, but deceptively so. Within his verse, he explores the vastness of both the African-American and the human experience, not for the academy, but for the masses. That's why his work—simple, honest, earnest, musical, radical and celebratory—crackles. It feels as if it was written this very day, for this moment.

Photography: Robert Kelley/The LIFE Picture Collection/Getty Images

LINUM

3
Architecture

LUCID

In Malta, an exploration of the architecture of Richard England—the fun uncle of Mediterranean modernism.

Photography by Romain Laprade & Styling by Camille-Joséphine Teisseire

DREAMS

Above: Rafael wears a shirt, trousers and belt by Givenchy.
Left: He wears a polo shirt by Charvet, with trousers and sandals by Hermès. Previous page: He wears a jacket by De Fursac.

Left: Rafael wears a shirt by Joseph, trousers by De Fursac and a belt by Givenchy.

Previous spread: Rafael wears a double-breasted jacket by Dior. Above and right: Rafael wears swimwear by Vilebrequin.

THE HISTORY OF UTOPIA

TEXT:
HUGO MACDONALD

Is utopian architecture a doomed quest to build human progress with bricks and mortar? Hugo Macdonald considers the philosophical value of visionary design—and catalogs its many real-world failures.

Is it possible to build heaven on earth? The word "utopia" was coined back in 1516 by Thomas More in his seminal book of the same title. More depicted in detail a fictional island with (what he considered to be) a perfect way of life. Derived from Greek, the word is portentously ambiguous, meaning either "a good place" or "no place." Too often, ambitions to achieve the former have resulted in something closer to the latter: Good places in theory frequently turn out to be no places to call home.

In history, utopias have often been associated with attempts by leaders with god complexes to assert power and control. Dictators aside, however, our quest for utopia is more commonly linked with our innate desire as humans for progress. In his anarchic essay, "The Soul of Man Under Socialism" (1891), Oscar Wilde stated: "A map of the world that does not include Utopia is not even worth glancing at, for it leaves out the one country at which Humanity is always landing. And when Humanity lands there, it looks out, and seeing a better country, sets sail. Progress is the realisation of Utopias."

What classifies an architectural project as utopian? Broadly, the word is used to describe attempts to—quite literally—build social progress. By virtue of this ambition, utopian projects are fundamentally concerned with new ways of living and sit toward the philosophical and political end of the architectural spectrum. This might mean dreaming up the single-family home of the future or building a new city from scratch.

Brazil's grand capital Brasilia was built in just 41 months between 1956 and 1960. It was President Juscelino Kubitschek's aim to build a city that represented a new future for the country, promising 50 years of progress in five. Oscar Niemeyer, together with urban planner Lúcio Costa, was commissioned to create a new

capital city replacing the former seaside capital of Rio de Janeiro. A UNESCO World Heritage site, the human endeavor of creativity, engineering and construction behind Brasilia is literally monumental. Niemeyer designed everything: from the magnificent Alvorada presidential palace to the government buildings, to the apartment blocks, right down to the bus conductors' uniforms. Brasilia had a clear utopian vision writ large in concrete: It represented a clean break from the corrupt, crime-ridden capital of Rio, presenting the population and the world with a modern capital city for a modern nation. However, Brasilia is a grim place to live. And herein lies a fundamental problem with so much utopian architecture: It doesn't leave room for people to live their own lives.

Shaped like an airplane, Brasilia is beautiful in plan. Individual buildings are impressive in photographs. Yet the city feels oddly distorted and uncomfortable at human scale. Wide planted boulevards and sidewalks, so generous in theory, are dusty and windswept, like an epic film set built more for camera angles than daily existence. The quality of life at street level is dire, with high rates of crime and unemployment. It is an urbanism case study for the dangers of designing with a bird's-eye view.

As an exercise in utopian architecture, the city stands as a stark warning of how difficult it is to build habitable progress at scale from scratch, too. In an interview with *The Guardian* on his 100th birthday, Niemeyer conceded: "It seemed as if a new society was being born, with all the traditional barriers cast aside. It didn't work. Now, Brasilia is too big. The developers, the capitalists are there, dividing society and spoiling the city. Brasilia should stop." But when urbanists criticized Niemeyer's top-down vision, he hit back: Most cities take centuries or even millennia to build up layers of

life, he pointed out. Niemeyer believed that he had designed the conditions for a city to develop over time, though notably, he kept his own penthouse studio in Rio, overlooking Copacabana beach.

Time might well be kind to Brasilia, but the same cannot be said for Robin Hood Gardens (1972) in Poplar, east London. The brutalist housing project by Alison and Peter Smithson was a utopian vision at a different scale from Brasilia, though no less didactic in its theoretical intent of using architecture to effect social mobility. It is currently under demolition, despite numerous attempts to save it in the decade since Tower Hamlets Council revealed it would cost £70,000 to bring each of the 214 apartments in line with modern living standards. As with Brasilia, the main problem lay with the disparity between the utopian vision and the built reality: People struggled to make their homes in Robin Hood Gardens.

The Smithsons were part of Team 10, a collective of left-wing, radical theorists that sought to redefine architecture and urbanism beyond modernism. After rigorous research into the future of housing, Robin Hood Gardens was their only realized social housing project. (Incidentally, they also won the commission for the British Embassy in Brasilia, though this was never built.) It had several successful elements, principally the domestic layout, beautiful and clever design details and the landscaping, which reduced the roar from the busy roads between which the buildings were wedged. It was their pioneering elevated walkways—"streets in the sky"—that brought about its downfall. These communal areas were intended to foster social cohesion among inhabitants as public spaces where people could come together, building a strong community. The streets in the sky became hot spots for vandalism and crime, and the project's reputation got trapped in a depressing cycle that perpetuated its demise.

Alison and Peter Smithson made their case in an extraordinary film for the BBC in 1970. They explained the ambition of their concept as: "A model, an exemplar of a new mode of urban organization... Its form will respond, we hope, to the way people want to live now. In a way, it will be like the first Georgian square in London. To the people who live in it, it offers a place with a special character, which will release them and change them and be capable of being lived in generation after generation." The householders' manual for inhabitants reads: "The Greater London Council and its architects have been working on Robin Hood Gardens since 1963; its builders since 1968; it is now your turn to try and make it a place you will be proud to live in." Besides obvious vandalism, reports by residents revealed intense frustrations that they could not inhabit these modern boxes as they had their previous row houses. They were too prescriptive.

The Smithsons' principled beliefs soon turned to indignation and dismay when they witnessed how their project was being treated: "It's very depressing for the builders, the contractors and the architects to feel that all the effort they put in is going to be smashed up," Peter sighs at one point in the documentary. While the architecture community rallied in favor of protecting Robin Hood Gardens as the embodiment of an important social housing experiment, an independent survey of residents claimed 75 percent supported plans for its demolition. The story of Robin Hood Gardens highlights the tense relationship architecture has between dogmatic doctrine and personal preference.

When we think of utopian architecture, we routinely return to the postwar period, hom-ing in on grand attempts to fix social housing and establish modernity from the wasteland of war. Rory Hyde is the curator of contemporary architecture and urbanism at London's Victoria and Albert Museum, which saved a three-story section of Robin Hood Gardens for its permanent collection. He explains: "The history of social housing is tied up with utopian ambitions to improve life for people and by extension society. This was said without irony, or any feeling of patronization for decades."

The postwar period—when there was a need for mass rebuilding—presented an opportunity to rethink how housing might be approached quickly, cheaply and efficiently, while meeting the needs and requirements of 20th-century family life. New materials, new industrial processes and new technologies gave birth to new ideas about what architecture could achieve. Architecture was, quite literally, a way to build something positive out of the destruction of war. The notion of utopia wasn't just a welcome relief, it was an escape. And yet, the excitement at the opportunity for rapid progress frequently left real people out of the picture. Postwar building programs, by virtue of their scale and the speed at which they were required, considered people in abstract numbers, reducing needs and behaviors to generalizations. Housing was a solution, a policy and a process, catering for the common denominator that would suit the greatest number of people. The Smithsons represented the culmination of a school of challenging thinkers in the field of architecture, that emerged in the postwar period and fizzled out in the 1970s. In their BBC documentary, Alison gives the impression that even she is growing cynical: "Society at the moment asks architects to build these new homes for [people]," she says. "This may be really stupid... We may be asking people to live in a way that is stupid. They maybe just want to be left alone." "Utopian housing projects in this period didn't often work," Hyde explains. "Looking back at what went wrong, it seems fair to say that a top-down singular vision was too rigid for reality. Life is more complex; people are not that straightforward." In the realm of 20th-century social housing, as with the building of a monumental new capital city, utopian aspirations are too tidy for the awkward messiness of human life. Building progress at scale inherently denies our self-determination as independent people with individual identities. So is utopian architecture inevitably doomed? "If we give up on utopias then, in a way, we give up on hope," Hyde says. "We just have to think a little differently from our postwar predecessors."

Stefano Boeri's Bosco Verticale (which translates to "vertical forests") in the Porta Nuova district of Milan is a contemporary architectural vision of utopia. The buildings certainly look utopian and radically different from the all-pervading grayness of a typical urban topography. Boeri, the president of La Triennale of Milan, has introduced nature and the notion of healthy buildings (for people, plants and the city) into urban architecture at scale. Completed in 2014, the two towers are home to more than 100 apartments, as well as 800 trees, 5,000 shrubs and 11,000 plants. The design, engineering and landscaping might have been complex but the intention is simple: The forests and vegetation convert a staggering amount of carbon dioxide into oxygen, simultaneously filtering pollution, reducing noise and naturally cooling and screening the apartments within. Boeri is cautious when asked if his ambition was utopian: "Our mission is to combine living nature with architecture," he explains. "I like to consider the trees as the tenants—the building supports life for the trees, as well as the people who live here. The plants are not an ornamental adornment. They are life for the building and the city."

Boeri describes the importance for architects to cultivate their obsessions. His own obsession with trees has many origins, including Italo Calvino's 1957 novel *The Baron in the Trees*, about a young boy who climbed up a tree and lived in the forest canopy for the rest of his life. His own vertical forests have certainly captured the imagination of planners and developers looking for a new model; he is working on 20 projects around the globe, from Cancun to China, São Paulo to Paris. There are even three forest cities in theoretical stages with sites in Mexico, Egypt and southwest China under discussion.

Boeri is careful to note that these are not cut-and-paste rollouts of the original blueprint that proved successful in Milan. Every subsequent vertical forest will be designed from scratch as a specific response to local social, natural and climatic environments. This elastic approach is, he believes, crucial in translating a big idea into a widespread reality. "When architecture is deterministic and presumptuous it becomes weak and does not work," he explains. "Architecture can act as a metaphor for progress. It requires systems and rules. But there must always be space left for real people and real life to flourish. Architecture can try to shape social behavior, but it's more likely that people will respond well to buildings if they feel they can evolve together."

The idea of nature, architecture and people in a mutually supportive communion, evolving synergistically, sounds like a 21st-century utopian standard. It feels more responsible and less bombastic, recognizing impact and evolution as fundamental components of progressive architecture. In northern California, there

is an interesting example of this relationship in action. The Sea Ranch is a 10-mile stretch of land on the Sonoma coastline, purchased in 1963 by an enlightened developer called Oceanic California Inc. Today it is an unincorporated community, comprising almost 2,800 lots on 3,500 acres that take in redwood forests, rolling hedgerows, fields and coastal sites. Development was planned and designed by Lawrence Halprin with architectural design prototypes originally established for condominium dwellings by Moore, Lyndon, Turnbull and Whitaker (MLTW) and hedgerow houses by Joseph Esherick. These were intended as guidelines, not blueprints, to inspire future dwellers to commission, design and build their own projects with respect for the land and their neighbors. A design review committee was established to catch any carbuncles.

As well as flexibility, what underpinned The Sea Ranch's success was a "constitution and a covenant" that engages inhabitants in an almost cultlike commitment to the overarching philosophy. This document goes into detail about the "rights, duties, privileges and obligations of all owners" safeguarding building-to-nature and building-to-neighbor relationships. "Living lightly on the land" is a core tenet: Architecture enters into a "territorial partnership" with nature, local building materials are "rough and simple" and structures are placed "within the land, not upon it." It sounds didactic but there has always been a fundamental understanding at The Sea Ranch that, in order to succeed, any guidelines have to be parameters more than rules. Inhabitants have to be able to design, build and inhabit their homes as individuals; personal homes are more likely than uniform housing to galvanize people around a common cause. The utopian vision requires people, as much as architecture, to build and shape it.

California photographer Leslie Williamson has made a career photographing the untouched homes of pioneering designers and architects. Her concern is to capture and reflect the soul of the inhabitant—not the aesthetic—of the home. She has photographed several homes in The Sea Ranch over the last decade and recognizes the careful balance here of the individual versus the entity. "The Sea Ranch is actually about homes, and that is why it works as a fairly utopian community; everyone might believe in the same ideals but everyone has their own unique home, too," she explains. "The problem with utopias is they tend toward the intellectual, and we struggle to nurture ourselves as individuals with ideas imposed on us about how we should live and behave. Architects with utopian ambitions don't tend to make easy homes to live in."

Good homes are vital for progress. The social and architectural standardization inherent in so many utopian plans is often their stumbling block because it renders life and people in unrealistic two-dimensional tidiness. It neglects the importance of home as a concept and misunderstands the core idea of what home represents. Homes are about individual expression, identity, safety, security. In *Parallel Utopias* (1995), Richard Sexton's rigorous study of The Sea Ranch, he notes: "A designer or architect can help you sort out your priorities but can never be a satisfactory surrogate inhabitant without you." Homes are personal, not intellectual; they become meaningful and powerful when they come from within, not above. "Let's not forget that for all of his grand visions," Williamson remarks, "the only home Le Corbusier built for himself was his perfect little wooden cabin overlooking the Mediterranean. It's a very different kind of utopia: more primal than modern."

beauty and possibilities of wood.

EXTRA LARGE:
Civilia
Ivor de Wolfe

Depending on who you ask, *Civilia* is a city plan, a polemical diatribe or a work of outstanding architectural collage. Subtitled "The End of Sub Urban Man," the 1971 book imagines a futuristic city—to be built on a site slightly east of Birmingham, UK—in which a million inhabitants might live in close-packed harmony.

Author Ivor de Wolfe (a pseudonym adopted by *Architectural Review* editor Hubert de Cronin Hastings) planned *Civilia* as a rebuke to the postwar town planners' infatuation with suburban expansion. "The need today is not to expand but to contract urban development," he writes, damning suburban houses as "Mindless little boxes that kipper the ground like the locusts they resemble."

De Wolfe's imaginary city makes dense habitation possible by having buildings on multiple levels —sometimes vaulting over each other—connected by escalators and pedestrian walkways. He illustrates his plans with lavish collages, a bricolage of interlocking brutalist blocks that jut out at improbable angles. The countryside, unspoiled by any further development, would be visible but rarely visited.

The critic Frederic Osborn—a leading advocate of the garden city movement—branded the project an "odious damned lie."

Was it all just a pipe dream? "Only for people who have wandered so far into a pathological state that common sense is bound to seem mad," de Wolfe insists.

A mountaineer in deep snow, long wooden skis over her shoulder, pushes up the last pitch of a steep ascent. Beyond, shards of the Alps rise tumultuously against a clear, cold sky. This view of Charlotte Perriand in the early 1930s, "face-to-face with the sky and infinity," as she described it, contrasts vividly with a much more widely published photograph of her resting elegantly on her tubular steel chaise lounge, face turned toward a pure white wall—a calculated depiction of repose and austerity. These images bracket two complementary aspects of Perriand and her work in modern design: She reveled in the raw contexts around her, discovering what she and her collaborators called *l'art brut*, but she also built places of refuge and comfort for people in them. This contrast, evident as much in the urbane interiors for which she became well known as in the mountain retreats she designed throughout her career, distinguished her from other modernists.

In one of her first professional projects, Perriand exhibited a small interior ensemble, "Bar Beneath the Roof," at the 1927 Salon D'Automne in Paris. Already prepared to find innovative projects at this event, people witnessed something profoundly different in Perriand's work. The proposed site, a cramped garret apartment, brought the space of struggling professionals and artists down to the elegant showrooms of the Grand Palais. With its spare, nickel-plated bar and stools, built-in phonograph, mirrored table and taut leather couch, the space expanded brightly under the bare, encroaching walls. The crisp geometries and reflecting light shaped a refuge from the din of the city below, a glimmer in the chaos of dirty roofs over Paris. An admiring critic, Paul Fiérens, declared that Perriand had come to sow "fruitful unease" among

Photograph: Junzo Inamura

her colleagues. Her interior proposed not only a contrast with the city but also hinted at the changing fortunes of young people in the precarious postwar economy—a point few of her art deco colleagues dared to make.

This bold project brought Perriand unexpected acclaim. "Overnight," she later recalled, "I went from being practically unknown to having camera bulbs flashing in my eyes." Just two years out of school, unsettled but exhilarated, she leveraged her opportunity and convinced Pierre Jeanneret and Le Corbusier to hire her as "an associate, responsible for the atelier's furniture and furnishings program." One of their first major collaborations, "Interior Equipment for a Dwelling" at the 1929 Salon d'Automne, immediately threw out a challenge. The term "equipment" implicitly repudiated the traditional distinction between interior decoration and architecture. The 950-square-foot apartment was shaped with standardized and tightly machined storage cabinets, rather than walls, and had tubular steel chairs and glass tables positioned in the severe space. Provocatively, even the bathroom flowed into the rest of the flat, its cabinets only selectively screening a bather from the dining table. A low, tiled partition holding towels on one side and a shelf for the bed on the other, similarly bridged spaces typically closed off from each other. Upon visiting the exhibit, Fabien Sollar, a critic for *Les Echos des industries d'art*, breathlessly complimented it for "an intrepidity that is impossible not to venerate." Another critic asked with less enthusiasm, "Are we, in the future, to disregard the smell and the noise for the sake of an interesting spatial creation...?" As architectural historian Mary McLeod argues, their space boldly proposed to do just that: to reshape domestic propriety in a world that offered people

In the early '60s, Perriand worked with Air France to modernize the company's London offices in accordance with its slogan at the time: "Air France at the point of progress."

"Overnight, I went from being practically unknown to having camera bulbs flashing in my eyes."

PERRIAND FOR POSTERITY

by Alex Anderson

The furniture Charlotte Perriand designed with Pierre Jeanneret and Le Corbusier in the late 1920s has remained in almost continuous production for nearly a century. Thonet manufactured the original models, and Cassina acquired rights to produce them for its *I Maestri* line in 1964; the company introduced Perriand's independent designs, including free-form tables, storage partitions and stools, in steel, plywood, bamboo, leather and plastic. The items of furniture pictured here come from Galerie Patrick Seguin, a Parisian specialist in 20th-century furniture that continues to do a roaring trade in Perriand originals alongside work by the three Jeans (Prouvé, Royère and Nouvel), and her collaborators, Le Corbusier and Jeanneret.

less space and fewer luxuries, but more freedom, than in the past.

Perriand's work over the next decade involved intensive research into low-cost dwellings. Traveling to Germany and Russia for the atelier in 1931, she witnessed disheartening privation and misery. In Frankfurt, she visited public housing blocks for the elderly. "A shiver still runs down my spine," she recollected, "it was a thoroughly sterilized place in which to die." In Moscow she saw a whole "population fantasizing about food in front of empty shops." When she returned to Paris she built compact, well-equipped student dormitories at the Swiss Pavilion and urban housing for the homeless in the Salvation Army Building. She also continued their work on minimum dwellings for the middle class. In a project Perriand directed at the 1935 Brussels World's Fair, "The House for Youth," she introduced an innovation shocking even among the modernists. Alongside a now standard rectangular storage cabinet, a painting by her close friend Fernand Léger, a whale vertebra and other found objects, Perriand exhibited a chair made of pine with a rush seat and back. When surprised colleagues asked her about such thoroughly un-modern materials, she said she "wanted to prove that one could work honestly in any material."

In later projects, Perriand experimented extensively with wood. For her own dining table, and for a desk commissioned by the editor of *Ce Soir*, she collaborated with Jean Chetaille, a craftsman and "a real wood lover," using thick slabs of recycled lumber, edges softened and surfaces unvarnished but rubbed smooth. She called these "free-form tables" because, as she put it, they would "master space" and create fruitful places for conversation and collaboration. Living in Japan and Indochina during the war, and later in Brazil, she developed versions of household equipment in bamboo, bent plywood and tropical woods. She exploited their unique capabilities, and affirmed, she later wrote, that "design flows from the materials and their use."

Perriand's research into material, minimum dwellings, the mastery of space with furniture, and her love of the mountains combined in a small but important project she developed with engineer André Tournon—a shelter for extreme alpine environments. They assembled it with an external tubular frame, prefabricated aluminum exterior panels and built-in plywood furniture. Unvarnished wooden interior walls would absorb and perspire the moisture of bodies and wet gear. Despite its extraordinarily compact plan—13 feet by 6½ feet—six people could comfortably store their equipment, converse, cook and sleep as the wind and snow raged outside. After exhibiting the shelter at the 1937 International Exposition in Paris, Perriand and her friends installed it on an exposed ridge facing Mont Blanc.

For much of her career after World War II, Perriand designed more substantial interior architecture for high mountain resorts at Méribel Les Allues and Les Arcs. At Méribel, she said, "the shortage of material sparked my imagination," as did mountain chalets nearby, rough furniture built by local craftsmen, and recollections of her comfortable but spare house in Japan. McLeod praised the resort—with its free-form tables, pine and rush chairs and beds, and built-in storage—for its "calm, simplicity, and rusticity." Beginning in 1967, Perriand worked for 20 years on the immense 40,000-bed mountain resort at Les Arcs. She and her team—including her close friend Jean Prouvé—thought of it as "an architectural laboratory" whose aim was to connect people with the snow and the mountains. They experimented extensively with compact interior equipment incorporating mass-produced bathrooms, integrated storage, desks and beds, and free-form tables. Perriand thought of each modest room as a comforting refuge for guests, their daily cares left momentarily behind and eyes cast—like a young mountaineer half a lifetime before—toward the icy, folded ridges of the distant Alps and infinity in the deep blue sky beyond.

Left Photography: Courtesy of Galerie Patrick Seguin

The

Inspired by the overcomplicated machines of Rube Goldberg, turn the pages to watch a flower—finally—get watered.

Chain

Photography by *Aaron Tilley* & Set Design by *Lisa Jahovic*

Reaction

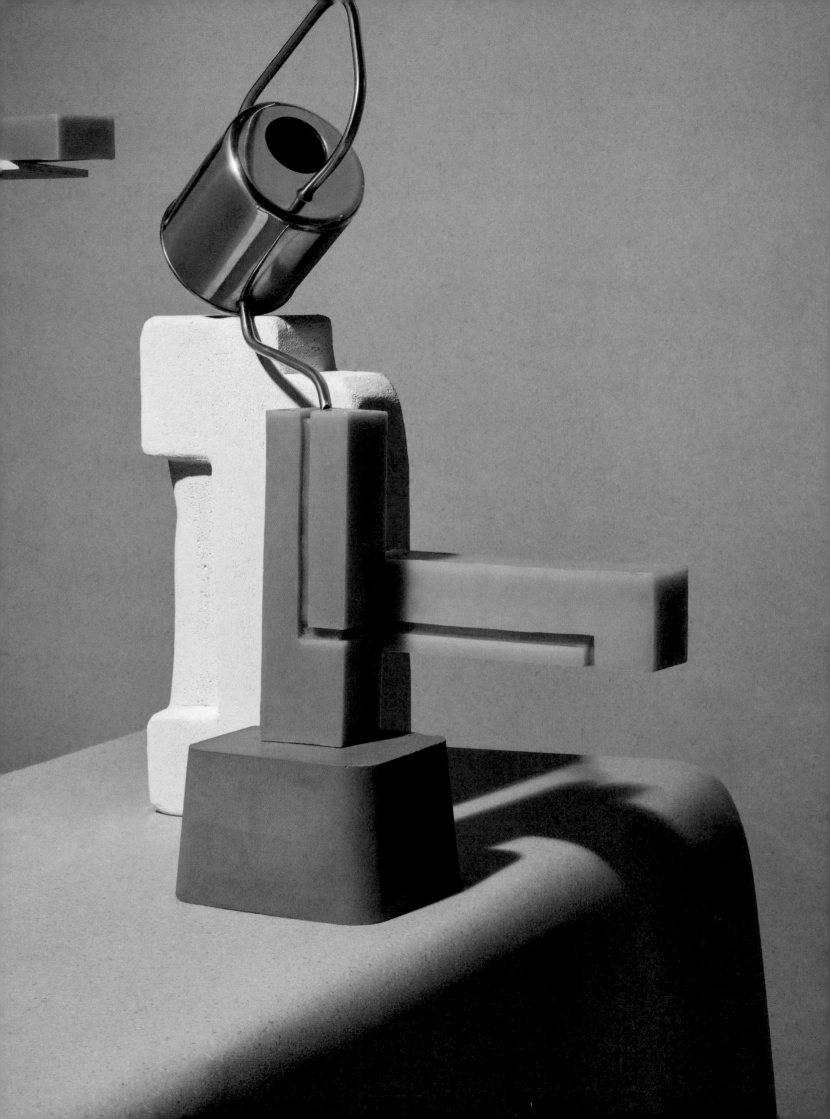

ARCHITECTURE

4
Directory

Photograph: Christian Møller Andersen

NIKOLAJ HANSSON

Salem Charabi

Meet the architect whose work flows from the Danish concept of *håndnær*.

Salem Charabi smiles a lot. He smiles as he greets you, he smiles when asked a question and he smiles when answering. While doing so, he exposes a charming gap between his front teeth and makes grand hand gestures to illustrate his words. Here, the architect-cum-designer discusses utopian architecture, running your own studio and infusing a bit of where you're from—in Charabi's case, Egypt and Denmark—into the things that you create.

When did you learn that you wanted to become an architect? I've always had a curiosity toward spaces and how they can make you feel a certain way. There's a saying that you forget what people look like and you forget what people say but you never forget how they made you feel. Becoming an architect has been a search to both understand and ultimately provoke that type of spatial experience.

The Danish design scene is highly competitive. What are you doing differently? I've always been drawn to buildings where every detail, from the door handle to the floor to the light, are all worked to equal perfection. I have a workshop in Nordhavn—an area in the northeast of Copenhagen—where I do all my work. There's this Danish term *håndnær*, meaning near to the hand. When objects are in your hands, you begin to acknowledge the techniques required to create them along with a growing appreciation of the material. This informs the design process at a far earlier stage, as opposed to starting out with a drawing and working your way forward from there. It's about forgoing the preconceived notion of the given object and instead taking an investigatory approach.

Can someone ever truly stand out if it is their conscious intention to do so, or is individuality something that arises as one progresses within a field? If one really seeks to make a difference within architecture, it shouldn't be about seeking the grand. It should be about going to a scale that is smaller than what we have gotten accustomed to in our highly industrialized world. Over time, one forms a far stronger sense of identity if seeking to answer the given conditions that are at hand, rather than heading straight for a grander utopia.

Does your Egyptian heritage influence your approach to design? There is a great difference in the ways that a highly industrialized country such as Denmark and a less industrialized country such as Egypt work. In Denmark, craftsmanship is exotic and gives added validation to objects, whereas in Egypt, it is far more innate in the culture. It is something that you do out of need—a reaction to the questions at hand. I have the appreciation from having roots in a place with a greater ease of means, making intuition play a much bigger role in how things are made, combined with the mythically beautiful Arabic aesthetic that is so deeply rooted within me. From both influences come the material and tactile appreciations. But even more, there is the aspect of memory—dedicating a little bit of where you come from to whatever you create.

What are the most boring parts of running your own studio? Logistics. They make up a lot of your daily workload when you're running an independent studio. The amount of phone calls and practicalities along with pushing for deliveries can be exhausting at times. The most boring part is undoubtedly spending time not creating.

How do the materials you use influence your design process? When you start to work with the actual material and its underlying meanings, you begin to realize why brick houses are red in some parts of the country and yellow in others. In the Middle East, the roofs are flat while in Europe, they're angled. Historically, this has been what has informed our architecture; the contexts of climate, the economy and culture that together shape the architecture of our inhabitance. In that lies a lot of poetry, taking every minuscule aspect into sincere consideration.

Would you say that you have a romantic relationship with architecture? Deeply, to the point of full-throttle emotionality. The romantic level is somehow connected to rediscovering an intimacy within what and how we create, rather than being nostalgic about the past or unrealistic about what I can achieve within my work. In that romanticized view of my work, it's about setting the best example for what I believe a profession should be.

"Since the birth of modernism, we've always worked with utopias in architecture," says Charabi, who advocates for a more pragmatic approach to design.

KATIE CALAUTTI

Object Matters

A pop history of Bubble Wrap.

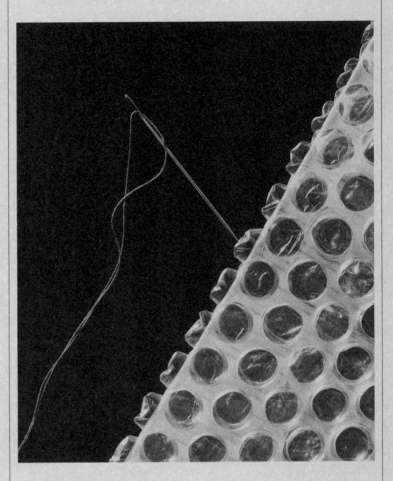

In the pecking order of packing materials, Bubble Wrap falls somewhere in the middle—above polystyrene peanuts, with their mess of static cling, but below environmentally friendly options like cornstarch packaging. But Bubble Wrap still reigns supreme when it comes to one thing: the delight factor that comes with finding it wrapped around shipped valuables, its air bubbles waiting to be popped.

Bubble Wrap wasn't originally intended for packaging. In 1957, New Jersey-based engineers Alfred W. Fielding and Marc Chavannes threw something at the wall—literally—and it didn't quite stick. After sealing a set of shower curtains, they grew excited by the ensuing air bubble-filled sheets of plastic and decided to market them as of-the-moment interior decor—meaning Bubble Wrap began as wallpaper. When that venture failed, they switched to pawning it off as greenhouse insulation—which turned out to be another misstep. They pressed on, and its true calling arrived when it served as the transport material for IBM's newly launched 1401 computer.

In 2006, the amount of Bubble Wrap manufactured in a year by Sealed Air (its parent company) could circle the equator 10 times. Since then, its status has deflated thanks to space-saving and cost-cutting shippers looking for more efficient alternatives. In response, the company invented collapsible sheets called iBubble Wrap. But the newly competitive product has one big downside for Bubble Wrap fans: The revamped version doesn't pop—when pressured, the trapped air simply redistributes within the sealed plastic.

Although traditional Bubble Wrap is becoming something of an obsolete offering, ingenious uses are still being found for it. Home security amateurs make a "Bubble Wrap burglar alarm" by laying sheets in front of doorways, Norwegian EMTs use it in hypothermia-prevention wrappings and some daring brides have even turned it into wedding dresses.

SECOND THOUGHTS
by Harriet Fitch Little

Bubble wrap isn't the only invention that sidestepped its original purpose. Mouthwash (Top: Mouthwash by Aesop) was intended for cleaning hospital floors and as a surgical antiseptic, because of its bacteria-killing properties. Tea bags (Center: Tea from A. C. Perch's Thehandel) were initially conceived as just the small silk bags that loose tea was to be sold in—until smart customers realised that the brew tasted a whole lot better if the leaves were actually left in the bag while dunking. Post-it notes (Bottom: Adhesive notes by Craft Design Technology) were a happy accident resulting from a scientist who, while trying to develop a super strong adhesive, accidentally created a super weak one instead. He shared his mistake with colleagues, one of whom used the weak glue to invent the Post-It note—a story that has been co-opted by management gurus as an example of how companies can learn from their mistakes.

Left Photography: goodhoodstore.com (Top), Christian Møller Andersen (Center and Bottom), Right Photograph: Aaron Tilley

Laura Waddell pays homage to *Anaïs Nin*: the erotic novelist who awoke desires in generations of young women—and became the patron saint of social media over-sharers.

LAURA WADDELL

Peer Review

In her own lifetime, Nin was better known for writing about other people than herself; Henry Miller and Gore Vidal were among the famous friends whose lives she chronicled in her published diaries.

When choosing a subject for my high school English dissertation, it was with glee that I paired Anaïs Nin's *Delta of Venus* with D.H. Lawrence's *Women in Love*, intent on shocking by writing on literary eroticism. I'd been put onto *Women in Love* by a gay friend a couple of years older. On a day we played hooky from school, he showed me the well-used VHS film adaptation, kept hidden from his father, and one thing led to another—as subversive art does. From an internet search of erotic literature, I plucked Anaïs Nin and began reading.

Her prose elicited such extremes of feelings: It was an experience as stimulating as rolling in a bed of velvet. In Anaïs' writing, sensuality gushes everywhere, spilling over. As a hormonal 14-year-old prone to weeping under the covers at midnight, I modeled my inner life on Anaïs' raw excessiveness.

Anaïs generously documented her own bisexual attractions. Of her intimate friend June, she wrote, "To think of her in the middle of the day lifts me out of ordinary living." She had darker preoccupations too, only in part reflecting the social standards of the day; her forays into fetish chase taboos into the darkest of corners, and she worried orgasm encouraged pregnancy, holding back from "radius and rainbows." Anaïs is excess in all things, every nerve rubbed raw, but as a woman in the 20th century, some realities pervaded.

The misfit maximalist with a penchant for masochism returns often to the theme of scooping up all pleasure a lifetime could offer. "I want to kneel as it falls over me like rain, gather it up with lace and silk, and press it over myself again," she said of happiness. Anaïs the sensualist, Anaïs the fantasist. And to what end? "Had I not created my whole world, I would certainly have died in other people's."

It is no surprise, then, that her book titles have been snapped up as provocative pseudonyms on every social media platform; entering her world is, for many readers, an introduction to one's own inner ecstasies.

Cult Rooms

Kenzo Tange fired up one of the 20th century's most ambitious architectural movements—but he kept his own home simple.

Kenzo Tange, the Pritzker Prize-winning Japanese architect and patron of the futuristic metabolist movement, had an ambitious vision for life in the mid-20th century. But it wasn't how he wanted to live at home.

Tange's most notable public works, including Hiroshima's Peace Memorial Park (1950), the Yoyogi National Gymnasium for the 1964 Tokyo Olympics, and a never-realized 1960 plan for Tokyo Bay, are all drama: soaring concrete mega-structures, undulating curves, artificial islands built on reclaimed land. They are rooted in grandiose, Marxian ideas of architecture and urban planning, and aim to satisfy the biological and spiritual needs of modern humans.

The house he designed for himself, constructed in 1953 in Tokyo, was smaller in scale and simpler in theory. Instead of building on lofty concepts for futuristic modalities, Tange looked to the past, repurposing an aesthetic from a millennium prior.

Tange's house—a main building situated behind a central plaza—could have been plucked right out of the 10th century. (The fanciest Heian-period courtyards would have included a carp-filled stream and pond styled to invoke the celestial paradise of the Amida Buddha, but the realities of 20th-century Tokyo real estate prices didn't allow for such luxuries.) The lines of the house were clean and straight. Angles were 90 degrees. Rooms were spare and modular, partitioned by paper sliding doors which could be opened or closed as needed. The entire structure was raised on wooden stilts to ventilate the rooms during Japan's summers, which were as sticky in the 1950s as they were 10 centuries prior.

Tange called the project The House, a utilitarian name for a space to be shaped in his own chameleonic image. The non-name was also a nod to the timelessness and transience of the building—an acceptance that houses like it were built before and will be built again. Although The House was a particularly stripped-back example of Tange's architecture, the same Heian-era principles that inspired it—a modular, unadorned, impermanent aesthetic—are writ large in the metabolists' most iconic buildings. In the 1960 metabolist manifesto that launched the movement, Tange's colleague Kiyonori Kikutake outlined a project called Ocean City: slabs of floating concrete, unmoored and free from national ties, would be home to industry, agriculture and entertainment for its residents. When they became dilapidated they would sink to the ocean floor.

The star project of the movement, the 1972 Nakagin Capsule Tower by Kisho Kurokawa, comprises dozens of micro-apartments encapsulated in concrete that can be joined together, then inserted or ejected from a central shaft. The tower still stands in Tokyo's Ginza neighborhood, though the majority of the capsules are uninhabitable, having fallen into disrepair. Community stakeholders are in a near-constant battle over its demolition. Shinto ideas

Tange's metabolist architecture was cited as the primary influence behind the futuristic design of Megasaki City in Wes Anderson's 2018 film *Isle of Dogs*.

of constant death and renewal of all things underpin Japanese aesthetic culture, both traditional and contemporary. "We are going to try to encourage active metabolic development in society through our proposals," Tange's collaborators wrote in their metabolist manifesto. The movement's very name anchors it to biological processes—cyclical, but with an expiration date. The Japanese word for metabolism, *kanji*, can also mean replacement, and renewal.

The House was torn down in the 1990s, to the chagrin of preservationists and nostalgists. But the demolition cleaves to a long history of ephemerality in Japanese architecture. Japanese vernacular houses are not built to last: Beams and foundations are wooden, roofs are straw and tree bark thatch, and walls are paper.

Japan's frequent earthquakes and resulting fires—common enough to be darkly referred to as the "flowers of Edo" in a popular saying, referencing the historical name for the city of Tokyo —destroyed noble and pedestrian houses indiscriminately. In Japanese aesthetic culture, the tragedy of life—and its great beauty —is that nothing stays the same for long.

Tange and the metabolists anticipated, and celebrated, inevitable change and eventual destruction, in projects both grand and personal. Tange's choice to invoke, in his own house, an aesthetic of the past was perhaps a reminder to himself of his place in time, and a gesture of reassurance that this was not the end of history.

DEBIKA RAY

Pipe Down

The day the muzak died.

If a tree falls in a forest and no one is there to hear it, does it make a sound? If elevator music stops playing and nobody notices, does it matter if it was ever playing at all? Your answer to the latter may depend on your propensity for anxiety: It's often said that music was first piped into elevators to calm the nerves of early passengers frightened about plummeting to their deaths.

Others say it was simply a way to entertain them. Certainly, this explains the enduring existence of background music in the public sphere. French composer Erik Satie is often credited with having invented the concept: Between 1917 and 1923, he wrote five pieces of what he called "furniture music," designed to "be a part of the surrounding noises"—heard, but not listened to. What is now referred to as "muzak," after the company that spent so much of the 20th century composing bland tunes for hotel lobbies and the like, is merely a specific type of aural pacification. It shares a common thread with "ambient," "lounge," "easy listening" and even the gentle indie rock you hear in trendy cafés.

Not everyone thinks it's so harmless. In 1992, UK environmentalist Nigel Rodgers founded Pipedown, the "campaign for freedom from piped music," claiming it was both irritating and bad for your health. The group achieved a major victory in 2016 when British department store Marks & Spencer banned muzak in its stores.

Indeed, background music can be manipulative. In its early days, Muzak patented Stimulus Progression, a style that gradually sped up in an effort to raise worker productivity. Train stations in several cities pump out classical music to discourage antisocial behavior. And Mood Media, the company that bought Muzak in 2011, now offers "sight," "sound," "scent," "social" and "systems" solutions— presumably in the belief that consumers more readily part with money when they are happy and comfortable. As psychologists Ronald Hill and Meryl Gardner explained in 1987: "Positive moods increase the probability that individuals will engage in behaviors with expected positive outcomes."

Background noise now goes beyond the aural. In the digital realm, we soothe ourselves by scrolling through a cacophony of memes on social media. And globalization is generating an aesthetic conformance that is the visual equivalent of background music—as everything from hotel lobbies to co-working spaces come to share a pleasing yet unremarkable lingua franca of post-industrial architecture, midcentury furniture and Nespresso machines. Perhaps in these troubled times— when the elevator cable of everyday life seems poised to snap—we yearn for a comforting soundtrack more than ever.

A PRESSING MATTER
by Harriet Fitch Little

You can't get an elevator door to close any quicker by using the "close door" button. No matter how often you press it, the doors will stay open for a pre-allocated length of time (based on how long it would take a disabled passenger to enter). Who on earth would design a "control" button that allows users to exert no actual control? According to Ellen Langer, they're there to give us the illusion of autonomy. "Doing *something* typically feels better than doing nothing," the Harvard psychologist told CNN last year. Apparently, the world is filled with useless buttons, with pedestrian crossings being the main offender: In New York City, only 100-odd of the 1,000 crosswalk buttons are currently functioning. Here are some buttons that actually work—we promise. (Top: Table lamp by Grässhoppa. Bottom: Mastercal calculator by Lexon.)

A taxonomy of tears.

Photograph: Laurynas Aravicius

OLIVER HUGEMARK

Sob Story

Tears are a touchy subject. Crying, especially in public, is often quickly followed by the impulse to excuse oneself.

In one sense of the word, of course, we are tearing up all the time. Basal tears—the thin film coating the eye and lubricating it round-the-clock—are endemic to all mammals. Every blink reboots this watery emulsion. Then there are reflex tears; the ones hardwired to swiftly wash out any wind-borne irritants. Without these stinging tears, chopping onions would no longer be a kitchen sink drama.

The third category, colloquially known as emotional tears, differ both in function and in chemical composition. The tears we cry when we are sad tend to contain higher quantities of hormonal proteins, including leucine-enkephalin—one of the body's many endogenous opioids. Perhaps it is the release of this natural painkiller that explains why bawling one's eyes out provides such a strong sense of cathartic relief, even joy.

Scientists know very little about the origins and meaning of emotional tears. (The hard-boiled Charles Darwin never got beyond understanding them in reflex terms: "We must look at weeping as an incidental result, as purposeless as the secretion of tears from a blow outside the eye," he wrote, and left it at that.) Emotional tears can't be explained away only as bodily reactions, however. Non-biological factors, such as relationship history and family background (and whether you've had a particularly terrible day), must be folded into the mix. But it is safe to assume that, like most emotional events, tears involve a labyrinthine reciprocity between internal conditions and external demands: To some degree we learn when—and how—to cry through socialization. Any stoic type can attest to that. This wiggle room between what we feel and what we do is, after all, the reason why the self-help industry continues to boom.

If you do start crying at a bad time, say on a first date at the movies, you might be left with no choice but to go all in: Burst into tears, pretending it's laughter, and pray it's your lucky night—and that your date catches a hit of the leucine-enkephalin–induced high as the tears trickle down your face.

Complete starred clues by getting your "house" in order.

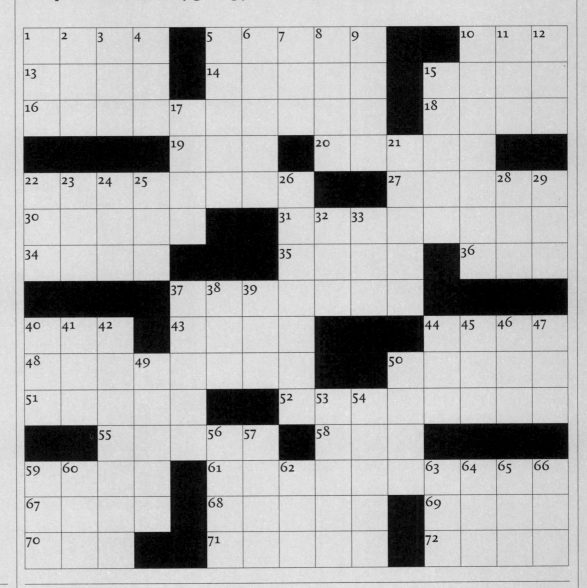

MOLLY YOUNG

Crossword

ACROSS

1. Epic tale
5. Part of a bikini or a purse
10. *Cowardly lad on "The Simpsons"
13. Words exchanged at a wedding
14. Get up
15. Lessen
16. *Virginia Woolf modernist masterpiece
18. Signs (or tattoos)
19. Unit of pointillism
20. Relaxed
22. El Al and Qantas, to name two
27. 71% of the earth's surface
30. Unrestrained
31. "Blue Velvet" actress Rossellini
34. Main character in Daniel Clowes' "Ghost World"
35. Kind of cabbage
36. Donkey
37. *David Mamet heist film (1987)
40. Shaggy animal whose Latin name is Bos mutus ("mute ox")
43. ____ grrrl (feminist punk movement of the 1990s)
44. Dirty books and magazines
48. Place to hear Muzak
50. Word that must be added to all starred clues, in keeping with this issue's theme
51. Frozen rain
52. Added on
55. Iron
58. Web address
59. Soul singer Redding
61. Nourishing winter meal served in a bowl
67. *Everyday, nothing special beverage served by restaurants
68. Screenwriter Sorkin
69. Cat also known as a mountain lion, cougar, or panther
70. Part of a chicken (or a piano)
71. *The fiddle leaf fig you keep forgetting to water
72. What jeans do if you cut them into shorts

DOWN

1. *Take care of someone's house while they're on vacation
2. Commotion
3. " What's Love ____ To Do With It" (Tina Turner jam)
4. Campfire byproduct
5. Social event famously hosted by Gertrude Stein
6. Cliché
7. 18-wheel truck
8. Arthur of 1970s tennis
9. Animal rights org.
10. Anti-apartheid revolutionary
11. Annoy
12. "____ Liaisons Dangereuses"
15. Work of art
17. Either of the two subjects of "Grey Gardens"
21. Buckwheat noodle varieties
22. *Tavern
23. Tiny charged particle
24. King in French
25. Topic in Michael Pollan book "How to Change Your Mind"
26. Singer married to Ava Gardner and Mia Farrow
28. "The New Yorker" critic Hilton ___
29. "Illmatic" rapper
32. Actor Shepard of "Paris, Texas"
33. Mimic
37. Give a speech
38. In good physical shape
39. Sticky ooze-y stuff
40. Seminal UK prog rock band
41. Everything
42. *Marilynne Robinson novel
44. Prodigal ___
45. Slang for coffee (or something that might get on your boots)
46. Function
47. Poet Hughes who was married to Sylvia Plath
49. Stanza in hip hop
50. "Inferno" is the Italian word for it
53. Wear
54. Type of shirt or dress fabric
56. Smack
57. Flippered marine mammals with whiskers
59. A group of this nocturnal animal is called a "parliament"
60. Ascot or bolo, for example
62. American pro-gun org.
63. Number on a bottle in your beach bag
64. *1982 hit Madness song
65. Mia in "Pulp Fiction"
66. Compensate

THE LAST WORD

Is it possible to anticipate the life span of a trend? To close the Architecture Issue, *Jonas Bjerre-Poulsen*—founding partner of Copenhagen-based Norm Architects and *Kinfolk* contributing editor—shares his tips for making design decisions that will stand the test of time.

You will always be a product of your time, whether you try to fight it or not. However, if I see something suddenly turn into a trend, I tend to be cautious of going down that route. I advise clients to invest in durable, simple, natural and timeless solutions when it comes to the main elements of interior architecture—walls, floors, ceilings and windows. The same goes for more expensive built-in elements like kitchens. Then you can always play around with the framework; with loose fittings, furniture, textiles and artworks, in order to make your space feel contemporary. After the global financial crisis in 2008, there has been a clear tendency to stray away from postmodernism in design and architecture, and a renaissance of natural and more minimal projects. In cultures of poverty, the artifacts seem to be simple, durable, natural and long-lasting. A timeless icon is something so simple that it makes very little noise in a space but has a design language that stands out. That very notion is reflected in our approach to architecture and design, where the main idea is to have spaces and furniture serve its user rather than be a means of artistic expression. We don't consider it a revolutionizing movement, but a subtle rebellion against the trend-driven. While aesthetics and technology have changed, basic tools of everyday life remain the same: A chair is still a chair, a glass is still a glass.

SPRING 2019

www.apuntob.it

Stockists

&TRADITION
andtradition.com

3.1 PHILLIP LIM
31philliplim.com

A DÉTACHER
adetacher.com

ACNE STUDIOS
acnestudios.com

APUNTOB
apuntob.com

ARJOWIGGINS
arjowiggins.com

ARMADILLO
armadillo-co.com

BANG & OLUFSEN
bang-olufsen.com

BEHOMM
behomm.com

CAUSSE
causse-gantier.fr

CHANEL
chanel.com

CHARVET
charvet.com

COS
cosstores.com

DE FURSAC
defursac.fr

DESIGN HOTELS
designhotels.com

DIOR
dior.com

EDIE PARKER
edie-parker.com

ERIK JØRGENSEN
erik-joergensen.com

ERMENEGILDO ZEGNA
zegna.us

FALKE
falke.com

GENEVA
eu.genevalab.com

GIVENCHY
givenchy.com

GUBI
gubi.com

HARLOW HENRY
harlowhenry.com

HERMÈS
hermes.com

HOUSE OF FINN JUHL
finnjuhl.com

J. M. WESTON
jmweston.com

JACQUEMUS
jacquemus.com

JAMES VELORIA
jamesveloria.com

JIL SANDER
jilsander.com

JOSEPH
joseph-fashion.com

KARIMOKU
karimoku.com

LAMBERT & FILS
lambertetfils.com

LAURENCE BOSSION
laurencebossion.com

LEFF AMSTERDAM
leffamsterdam.com

LINDBERG
lindberg.com

LINUM
linumdesign.com

LOEFFLER RANDALL
loefflerrandall.com

MANSUR GAVRIEL
mansurgavriel.com

MARIMEKKO
marimekko.com

MARSET
marset.com

MUGLER
mugler.ca

MUTINA
mutina.it

ODE TO THINGS
odetothings.com

PARACHUTE HOME
parachutehome.com

PAUL SMITH
paulsmith.com

ROCHAS
rochas.com

ROSIE ASSOULIN
rosieassoulin.com

ROYAL COPENHAGEN
royalcopenhagen.com

SAINT LAURENT
ysl.com

SAMSØE & SAMSØE
samsoe.com

SAMUJI
samuji.com

SHAQUDA
shaquda.jp

STETSON
stetson.com

STRING
string.se

THE KOOPLES
thekooples.com

TINA FREY
tinafreydesigns.com

VILEBREQUIN
vilebrequin.com

WALLPAPERSTORE*
store.wallpaper.com

WHITE BIRD
whitebirdjewellery.com

Behomm
Community

Home Exchange for Creatives and Design Lovers

TRAVEL STAYING FOR FREE AT HOMES OF CREATIVES

1. REGISTER WITH YOUR HOME.
2. CONTACT A HOME YOU LIKE. AGREE ON DATES.
3. STAY AT THEIR HOME FOR FREE WHILE THEY STAY AT YOURS.

BEHOMM.COM

ISSUE 31

Credits

COVER
Photographer
Romain Laprade
Stylist
Camille-Joséphine Teisseire
Grooming
Taan Doan
Model
Rafael Mieses
Photography Assistant
Esteban Wautier
Casting
Sarah Bunter

Raphael wears Hermès
head-to-toe

P. 32 - 33
Photograph: ©*Richard Serra*
/ Artists Rights Society
(ARS), New York. Photo:
Lorenz Kienzle. Courtesy of
Gagosian

P. 60 - 105
Photographer
Luc Braquet
Stylist
Camille-Joséphine Teisseire
Hair
Taan Doan
Makeup
Cyril Laine
Model
Mamadou Lo
Model
Loane Normand
Production
Western Promises
Casting
Sarah Bunter

P. 71
Top right: *Mamadou*
wears a suit by Paul Smith,
socks by Falke and shoes
by J.M. Weston
Bottom right: *Loane* wears
a dress by Dior, stockings
by Saint Laurent and
carries a bag by Celine
Bottom left: *Mamadou*
wears a suit by Samsøe
& Samsøe, a rollneck by
De Fursac and a belt by
J.M. Weston

P. 126 - 137
Photographer
Romain Laprade
Stylist
Camille-Joséphine Teisseire
Grooming
Taan Doan
Model
Rafael Mieses
Photography Assistant
Esteban Wautier
Casting
Sarah Bunter

P. 152 - 157
Ceramic tiles from the
Rombini and Primavera
collections by Mutina

P. 182 - 183
Photograph: *Kenzo Tange*
© Michiko Uchida

Special Thanks:
Antonio Barrientos at St.
George's Park Hotel
Jacques Barsac
Elite Paris
Richard England
Fosbury & Sons
Le Vauban, Paris
Le Voiturium, Paris
Louis Galea
Justas Studio
New York City Center
Nicolas Martin at Western
Promises
Pernette Perriand